Living Fearlessly Through Fasting and Prayer

Living Fearlessly Through Fasting and Prayer

Jennifer LaCharite

LIVING FEARLESSLY Through Fasting & Prayer by Jennifer LaCharite

ISBN: 978-1-59755-640-8
Published by: ADVANTAGE BOOKS™, www.advbookstore.com

LIBRARY OF CONGRESS CONTROL NUMBER: 2021950499

NAMES: LaCharite, Jennifer, Author
TITLE: LIVING FEARLESSLY Through Fasting & Prayer
Publisher Advantage Books
IDENTIFIERS: 9781597556408 (print)
SUBJECTS: RELIGION: Christian Life – Inspirational
RELIGION: Christian Living – Prayer
SELF-HELP: Motivational & Inspirational

First Printing: December 2021
21 22 23 24 25 26 10 9 8 7 6 5 4 3 2 1

Acknowledgements

To my Heavenly Father, thank You for giving me the idea to write this book. Thank You Lord for all the blessings in my life; my family, health, friends, career, and the gifts and talents that with which You have generously gifted me. And more importantly, I thank You, for your forgiveness of my sins, past, present, and future. I hope and pray that this book is a blessing to many and draws Your people to a personal and intimate relationship with You.

I wish to express my deepest appreciation to my family, first to my son, Jake Jackson. Jake, you are one of the greatest blessings in my life. Having you changed my life. The love I have for you is fierce and unconditional. Every time I hear you call me Mom, my heart melts. You are a wonderful young man, daring, strong, kind, and giving. Thank you, Jake, for all your support and encouragement. You are always quick to remind me to trust God no matter what. Your continual reminders to not worry but instead pray about it and hand it over to God, has gotten me through times of uncertainty. You always made it sound so simple, and you are the only person I know that lives it out. I am so proud of the man you are becoming. You are highly favored and I know God is going to do great things through you.

To my dad, Ronald Thayer, thank you for your support, encouragement, and patience. Dad, you are the greatest man I know. Since I was a little girl, I looked up to you. One memory that will always remain with me is when I was a little girl, I enjoyed hanging out with you in your home office while you worked. I remember finding an entrepreneur magazine lying around your office, and I latched on to that. As I held onto that magazine, I told myself one day I would become an entrepreneur and own my own business just like my dad. Thank you, Dad, for your unconditional love and the patience you express not only to me but to many others. Thank you for believing in me and not allowing me to give up when things got tough. Every girl wants to know she will always be daddy's little girl, even as an adult. I am beyond grateful for the close relationship we have.

To my stepdad, James Chambers, and my mother, Audrey Chambers, a big thank you for all you have both done for my son and me. No matter what path I found myself on, you two have always been supportive. I am truly grateful for both of you being open when I needed advice. More than anything, I cannot express this enough, but thank you both for showing all of us how to live a selfless life. You are two of the most unselfish people I know. Mom, I want to thank you for showing me at a young age that prayer changes everything. You kept that plaque on the wall in our kitchen that said, "Prayer Changes Everything." You taught me at a young age that anything was possible. Your confidence in me is one of the reasons I am where I am today.

To my sister, Michele Desmond, thank you for always being one of my biggest cheerleaders. You remind me often that with Jesus, nothing is impossible. You are an inspiration to many, and just like our parents, you are so incredibly giving and selfless. The bond between Sisters is one of the greatest blessings from God. I look up to you in many ways, Sis!

Table of Contents

Introduction

LIVING FEARLESSLY Through Fasting & Prayer is book one of a series that covers how to live a fearless life as God intended for us too. In this book, the reader will discover how spiritual fasting and prayer can help any believer have complete victory over any area of their life. Fasting is one of the least practiced Christian disciplines. Yet, it's one of the most powerful means to achieving prosperity and breakthrough in our lives. We live in a fallen world that is full of darkness, hardship, hurt, and sorrow. Being a believer in Christ does not mean you are immune to the trials and temptations of this fallen world. If you want to learn how to overcome fear, worry, addictions, depression, having lack in your life, how to pull down strongholds in your life, then LIVING FEARLESSLY Through Fasting & Prayer is an excellent start.

In this book, I will share what biblical fasting is, the benefits of fasting and prayer, the power of fasting and prayer, how you can receive a breakthrough by fasting and prayer, and how you can incorporate fasting into your everyday life. I will also share many personal testimonies throughout the book and include some recipes I have used during my fasts. This book is largely about my journey of fasting and what I have learned. I do not claim to be an expert in spiritual fasting or being a believer of Christ. But, I can share with you what God has revealed to me and how He has worked in my life through my time spent in prayer, in fasting, and by reading His Word. The more time I spent doing all the above, the more God revealed Himself to me. And the more I wanted to learn what it takes to live a fasted lifestyle.

I want to share with you how this book came about and parts of my journey that led me to where I am today. Since 2017, I began to have this intense stirring in my spirit that there had to be more to this thing we call life. I have lived a pretty good life, so this stirring in my spirit was not because I was depressed or unhappy with my life. One day while praying, I asked God if this was really all there was to life? We go to college, raise our kids, work, pay bills, grocery shop, cook, work out, meet up with friends, go to church on Sundays, and do it all over again.

The stirring within me was fierce. The best way to explain this is that I felt like I was about to explode from the inside out if God did not show me that there was more to life than what I was experiencing. One day, while in prayer,

I told the Lord, if there is nothing more, then why not take me home right now? Please understand this, I love my son, family, and friends, and I still enjoy my career after 21 years. At this point, I had accomplished most of what I set out to do, but there was this thing stirring within me that would not go away. I wish I could say that God revealed what that more was immediately, but it would be a while later before I learned what it was.

About a year after I first started to have this strong stirring in my spirit, my son mentioned that he would like for us to move to California. I never thought I would move to California. I had visited it a few times and was never impressed. But for some reason, at that moment, I did not hesitate. I said, "Let's do it." Within eight months of my son bringing this up, we sold our condo, sold everything, gave away a lot, and moved to Southern California. Keep in mind that I was also leaving behind all that I knew and a successful real estate business that took me years to develop. After our first year in California, the pandemic hit us. We were in lockdown, and I was away from all that I knew. My family, friends, my home of 46 years, so it was a bit unsettling.

Seven months before our move, I had a vision while in prayer one morning. I saw myself sitting on our deck overlooking the pool and the ocean. I was sitting in a white shabby chic oversized chair with my feet resting on an ottoman. My notebook, laptop, pen, and coffee sat on the side table next to me. I felt the Lord showing me that I would be writing. This came as a surprise to me because I don't ever recall having a desire to write. Almost a year after our move, I was on a multi-day fast and began researching more about the benefits of fasting. The more I learned, the more excited I became and knew I had to share this information.

To be clear, I do not have a home on the ocean yet. But, as I write, I am sitting in my white down feather, shabby chic, oversized chair, with my feet resting on the ottoman, with a peek-a-boo view of the ocean from my living room and balcony. I mentioned that I had visited California a few times and was not impressed. But, today, I can say I am in love with California. The downtime that the pandemic brought upon us allowed me to focus on this book and spend a lot of time praying. Fasting and prayer are just one of the many things we can do as believers to draw closer to the Lord.

At some point, all of us have and will continue to experience trials that may feel debilitating. Whether it be financial troubles, depression, sickness, or disease, the list is endless. The truth is God wants to bless you, and He wants you to have complete victory over your trials. He wants you to live life abundantly and be prosperous in every area of your life. He wants you to overcome many of the trials or temptations you face; it will require complete dependence upon God. Your total dependence upon God will give you direction, strength, and peace during trials.

The Bible is the most powerful book in the world. It is a God-breathed book; it is a spiritual book. This is a truth that many do not fully comprehend, and it's one of the reasons why so many people are not seeing breakthroughs. The words in the Bible are alive and very powerful. It is unlike any other book in the world. It was God's Word that created the heavens and the earth and everything in them, and it was His breath that gave us all life. That should open your eyes to just how powerful the words of God are. Once you begin to understand the power behind speaking God's promises over your life or your family, it will change your life. The Bible is full of God's promises for our lives; you have to be willing to read the Bible and learn how to apply them to your life today.

Praying God's Word along with fasting over your circumstances produces victory a lot quicker than any other approach will. No matter what is going on in the world or around you, you can have faith and confidence, knowing that God's promises are for you today. Not for some time in the future or once you get to Heaven but for today. The Bible says that faith comes by hearing and hearing the Word of God. How can you have faith if you are not reading the Word of God? If you are reading the Word of God, then you should know how important it is to fast.

Many will take the time to pray, but not many spend time fasting. Fasting is a Christian discipline that every believer should be doing. In the Bible, Jesus said, *when* you fast, He did not say *if* you fast. Jesus was implying that fasting should be an essential Christian discipline and it would become a necessity after He ascended to Heaven. Jesus's fasting was an example of how we can overcome difficult situations we will all face in this life.

Fasting and prayer is a powerful Christian discipline. It will help you draw nearer to God and break the chains of bondage, addictions and undo the heavy burdens in your life. Fasting and prayer will help you to become a fearless believer. My life is blessed, but it has not been without its struggles. It was not until I began to spend more time reading the Bible that I began to wonder why

I was not experiencing this peace and prosperity that is talked about so much in the Bible in my own life.

This led me down a long journey of seeking more of God regarding His promises for His children. The more I studied the Bible, the more I realized that I could obtain victory over circumstances in my life by fasting, prayer, and putting on the full armor of God. I grew up in church, but fasting was not talked about much in the churches I attended. Even today, fasting is not taught in-depth within our churches. Some of the churches I attended did call for a corporate fast for one reason or another. Although I had participated in them, honestly, I did not completely understand the purpose of fasting.

Throughout the years, I tried an occasional fast here and there on my own, but I do not recall any specific breakthrough. It certainly was not because fasting does not work. It was because I did not know what I was doing. I did not understand that prayer and fasting go hand in hand. More importantly, I did not use that time to devote to God. I am thankful for my upbringing and grateful for the church leaders that were a part of my young life. But I can't help but wonder how different my life may have been if someone had taught me what it meant to have a personal relationship with Jesus. Or how different things may have been had I understood the importance of fasting, prayer, and reading the Word of God, the Bible.

I am grateful for the life experiences I've had. But today, I am thankful for understanding the importance of having an intimate relationship with Jesus Christ. And I am comforted in knowing that God does speak to us, and we can hear His still small voice. For years I allowed my circumstances to define who I was because I did not know who I was in Christ. It is a lot easier for us to identify with who we are when things are going great. For me, it was graduating from college while working full-time and being a single mommy to a newborn baby boy.

Later my identity became more focused on real estate, which was the career path I took—and later, opening my own businesses. But there were rough patches when my whole world was shaken. Like when my bank account was overdrawn, my electricity was shut off in the middle of winter, and I had several real estate deals fall through within the same week. It took me a long time to realize that just because I am a Christian does not mean that I will not experience major challenges throughout life. I had this false sense of identity and a false sense of security.

Through some of the most challenging times in my life, I learned my identity is not in what I accomplish. My security is not in how much money I have in the bank. It was during those dark moments when I was crawled up in a ball on the floor crying so hard that my heart hurt that drove me to seek God. I knew there had to be a better way. The more time I spent with God in prayer and reading the Bible, I began to understand that our circumstances do not define who we are.

During one of my seasons of fasting, it occurred to me that there are many people out there just like me seeking for a breakthrough in some area of their life. Maybe you are like me and have tried everything you could think of; begged God, repented, spoke positively over your circumstances, prayed for hours on end only to be left feeling hopeless. I have learned that sometimes prayer is not enough. God has led me on a journey to seek Him with all my heart. Part of that included adding fasting as one of the many Christian disciplines I live out. By sharing my story and what the Lord has revealed to me, I hope that this book will encourage you to seek God with all your heart and soul.

Why I chose the lion for my front cover

The Bible uses many metaphors to describe Jesus. For example, in the Bible, Jesus is called the Lamb of God to illustrate His gentleness, but He is also called the Lion of the tribe of Judah to illustrate His absolute authority and power over all of creation. In Revelation 19:16, the lion symbolizes Jesus as the conquering king of kings, a roaring lion taking vengeance on His enemies. In Ezekiel 10:14, the lion is described as one of the cherubs surrounding God's throne. Lions are legendary for their courage, strength, beauty, and fearlessness.

Lions arc bcautiful, but they can also be a force with which to be reckoned. There is beauty in both the sheep and the lion, and there is a time for gentleness and a time for fearlessness. One of my mottos in life is to "Be Strong," which was on my license plate for years. I always thought of the lion's attitude when I reminded myself to be strong no matter the circumstances. Lions lead while sheep are followers. The lion is confident and decisive, while followers are indecisive. A lion attitude is not concerned with fitting in or concerns themselves with what others think they should be doing.

A lion does not blend in. They shine. A lion hungers for its mission in life and refuses to drift through life. A lion does not waste their time with talk. They walk the talk. Lions are doers, not just dreamers. Lions do not give up, and no matter how tough things get, they keep going. A lion represents courage and fearlessness, and my book series is on LIVING FEARLESSLY.

Chapter One

What Is Biblical Fasting?

Biblical fasting is a spiritual discipline that was encouraged by Jesus. Fasting is mentioned in both the Old and New Testaments and mentioned more than 50 times in the Bible. It is defined as abstaining from food for spiritual purposes. Unlike fasting for health reasons, Biblical fasting requires an attitude of seriousness, sincerity, and, most of all, humility. Before Jesus began His ministry on earth, He fasted for forty days and forty nights. As soon as Jesus was baptized, he went up out of the water. At that moment, heaven opened, and He saw the Spirit of God descending like a dove and alighting on him. And a voice from heaven said, *"This is my Son, whom I love; with whom I am well pleased."* (Matthew 3:16) Then Jesus was led by the Spirit into the wilderness to be tempted by the devil. After fasting forty days and forty nights, He was hungry. (Matthew 4:1-2)

When Jesus was led into the wilderness to be tempted, He knew He would face every difficulty known to mankind. To have the strength to overcome every situation, He knew He needed to fast. If Jesus was led to fast, wouldn't it make sense for us to fast too? Some may argue that Jesus fasted because He was preparing for ministry. This is true, but His fasting was also an example of how we can overcome difficult situations we will face in this life. It's not a matter of if we will face difficult times, it's when. We live in a fallen world ruled by the prince of the air, Satan.

The enemy's only purpose is to kill, steal and destroy. One of Satan's greatest lies is to have people believing that he does not exist. If you question whether he exists, look at the world we are living in right now. The hate, anger, and deception that is all around us does not come from our all-loving Almighty God. I remember at a young age learning about Satan. I was terrified of him yet naively felt sorry for him and wondered if there was any chance of Satan getting saved. I think I even prayed for his salvation when I was a child. The Bible is very clear that Satan is an enemy of every believer. One might hope that Satan would have mercy on us when he sees that we are struggling, but that is not how he operates. Rather that is when he presses in even more.

At a young age, I remember my pastor explaining that we became a target of Satan's once we became saved. Can you imagine the fear that was instilled into my young mind? For years that concerned me enough to cause me to shy away from sharing the Gospel. As I matured in Christ, understanding that we were created in the image of God and have authority in Christ, that fear was turned into confidence. Fasting and prayer opens the door for God to reveal who He is and His character. One of the most extraordinary things that fasting has done in my life was to show me that I can rely upon and trust God to give me the strength to carry out my time of fasting.

Fasting is one of the quickest ways to assume a humble heart. The reason I bring this up is because I believe that many of us think we are humble. Or at least I did. During one of my fasts, one of the things the Lord revealed to me was that not reaching out to others for help is a form of pride. This is important because sometimes our prayers or breakthroughs are not happening because of pride or unforgiveness in our hearts. Nevertheless, nothing is hidden from the Lord.

A while back, I was going through a situation. My family pulled together and surrounded me with love, support, and help. I have always had a close and loving relationship with my family. Still, it was not until this situation that I realized my family knows when I need their help, even though I may not recognize it myself right away. I felt so loved, thankful, and yet astonished at how quickly they surrounded me without me having to ask for their help. As I shared this astonishment with my parents, they both told me that is what family does. Up to this point, and I was in my early 40's I was never quick to ask for help. Asking for help was not something that crossed my mind because I was so used to doing everything on my own. Not too mention, I did not want to be a burden to others. It was later revealed that this is also a form of pride, even if it seemed to be unintentional.

My point in sharing this is that pride is not always about being arrogant. When we are fasting, we are willingly depriving our bodies of all pleasurable food. It is a significant portion of our day if you think about how much time we spend thinking about food, preparing our food, and eating. It would make sense that while our bodies are being deprived for the purpose of drawing nearer to God, He will draw near to us. The Bible says that man shall not live by bread alone. When I started to take fasting seriously, I had a new understanding of what it meant that man should not live by bread alone. It was hard for me to go many days without food. The first few days, my stomach hurt, and I was tired. By the third or fourth day, I was no longer focused on depriving myself. My focus shifted from my hunger pains to the Lord. My focus shifted from myself to the Lord. That is when the concept of man shall not live by bread alone became real because I was drawing on God's strength through prayer rather than on my own strength. Because our bodies require food for sustenance when we are fasting, it's important to keep our hearts and minds focused on God. This is so that He may be the full source of our strength during our period of fasting. God promises that when we seek Him with all our heart, we will find Him. What better way to seek Him with your whole heart than by fasting?

When Jesus was questioned by the disciples in Matthew 9 why the Pharisees and they, the disciples of John, fasted often but Jesus's disciples did not, Jesus answered, *"...Can the friends of the bridegroom mourn as long as the bridegroom is with them? But the days will come when the bridegroom will be taken away from them, and then they will fast."*

What Jesus was saying is that fasting would become a necessity after He ascended. While Jesus was here on earth, His followers delighted in a close fellowship and friendship with Jesus. Before Jesus sent His disciples out to minister, He bestowed upon them power and authority over unclean spirits to cast them out and to heal all kinds of sickness and disease. (Matthew 11) It is no different for us today than it was for Jesus's disciples after He ascended. Fasting is a necessity.

In Luke 22:35, Jesus asked His disciples, *"When I sent you without purse, bag or sandals, did you lack anything?' 'Nothing,' they answered. He said to them, "But now you have a purse, take it, and also a bag; and if you don't have a sword, sell your cloak and buy one."* Jesus was instructing His disciples that after His departure, the entire dynamic would change. He would no longer be on earth to physically prepare His disciples and provide provision for them. In other words, they would need a different type of preparation, and fasting would be a vital part of this new preparation. Fasting should be a vital part of our preparation as well. In Matthew 6:16-18, Jesus says, *"When you fast do not look somber as the hypocrites do, for they disfigure their faces to show men they are fasting. Truly, I tell you the truth, they have received their reward in full. But when you fast, put oil on your head and wash your face, so that it will not be obvious to men that you are fasting, but only to your Father, who is unseen; and your Father, who sees what is done in secret, will reward you."*

It is also written in the Bible that what is done in private, God will reward publicly. This is similar to the verse in Matthew 6 that tells us not to do our charitable deeds before men, to be seen by them. Otherwise, you have no reward from your Father in heaven. Fasting and our charitable deeds require a humble heart. When people announce their fasting or charitable deeds for their friends and family to see, they are doing so because they seek man's attention and affirmation. This is not of a humble heart. Of course, there will be times you need to share with your family or friends that you are taking time to fast and pray, especially if you live with others.

Jesus was making the point that you don't need to announce your fast for everyone to know. This is between you and Him. Notice in Matthew 6, Jesus said, *"When you fast..."* For Jesus, it was a matter of *when* believers would fast, not if they would fast. Jesus is implying that fasting should be an essential Christian discipline. It would be no different than when Jesus spoke the words, *when* you give to the needy or *when* you pray. Jesus expected that we would give to the needy, pray and fast.

The early disciples made fasting a vital part of their ministry. Many of their ministries started after they fasted. Biblical fasting is linked with times of prayer, and the more serious we approach fasting and prayer, the more serious our results will be. Wouldn't you like to see more serious results in your life? I will be the first to tell you that fasting is by no means easy. But what discipline is easy? As with any other discipline, once you see the results, the more you look forward to it. The benefits and rewards from fasting will motivate you to want to do it even more.

There are things that we cannot do on our own strength. For some, it may be breaking free from bad habits. While others may feel they don't hear from God, or they do not receive divine revelation while reading the Bible. That was a biggie for me. I knew in my heart I needed to read the Bible more on my own, but honestly, I thought it was boring. I wanted to like reading the Bible and wanted to understand it. Still, I did not understand how what happened thousands of years ago would help me today. Fasting is one of the things that heightened my understanding of the Word of God.

I now receive what I refer to as, supernatural revelation of the Bible. I share this because there are answers in the Bible to almost every problem or situation you will face in this lifetime. The Bible is not just a book about the stories of people from the past. It's full of answers, insight, and direction for our lives. Fasting also suppresses our flesh, which will help you receive divine revelation from the Lord. You cannot receive this kind of revelation from your own carnal mind. It's a spiritual kind of revelation that only comes from the Holy Spirit.

When you suppress your flesh, you are telling your body that it does not have control over you. You are telling your flesh no and saying yes to God. This is important to understand because it is our spirit that has a connection with God. So often, our spirit is weighed down by the flesh and by the things of this world. Too often, when God does speak to us, we cannot hear Him because our flesh may be weighed down by worry or our emotions. By subduing the flesh through fasting, you will learn to walk in the spirit and communicate with God through spirit.

God is spirit, and we are made up of spirit, soul, and body. Our body being the physical body, our soul being our mind, will, emotions & conscience, and our spirit. When you were born again, you were given a brand-new spirit through Christ. Old things passed away and all things became new in your spirit. God put His anointing power on the inside of you. God has already given you everything you will need in your born-again spirit. But it's up to you to renew your mind, so you can learn how to release what God has placed on the inside of you. You will not see a manifestation of power or victory released in your life until you start renewing your mind. This is only done by reading the Word of God. God's Word is spirit and life, and it reveals spiritual reality.

In John 6:63, Jesus said, *"The Spirit gives life; the flesh counts for nothing. The words I have spoken to you, they are full of the Spirit and life."* Therefore, fasting is so important because it suppresses the flesh. I believe this is why it is hard for some people to understand the Bible. If you are walking in the flesh, you will not receive the supernatural revelation and understanding of His Word. Biblical fasting is abstaining from food in order to redirect your attention to God. It is a powerful way for Christians to deepen their relationship with God. It is an opportunity to set aside other things while preparing yourself to seek God's face and hear His voice.

Chapter Two

What Fasting Is Not

As I began to study and seek the Lord for an understanding of biblical fasting, I have concluded that a biblical fast is abstaining from food. While other fasts may include giving things up like television, social media, or chocolate, it is my opinion those are not true biblical fasts. However, I know the Lord is more interested in your heart than a religious act, according to Isaiah 58. If the Lord has called you to fast something for a certain period, then listen to God!

The Hebrew word for fast is *tsom*, and the literal translation means "no food." In Greek, fasting means *nesteia*, and it means the voluntary "abstinence from food." According to Baker's Evangelical Dictionary of Biblical Theology, fasting is an abstinence from food and or drink as an element of private or public religious devotion. According to the Bible, fasting is an expression of personal devotion linked to three major kinds of life crisis: lamentation/penitence, mourning, and petition. Without exception, it has to do with a sense of need and dependence, of abject helplessness in the face of actual or anticipated calamity. Fasting is not a means to manipulate God or to twist His arm. I will explain more on that a bit later. When fasting is done with a pure heart and pure motives, the biblical way, God does respond.

Biblical fasting is also not a means for weight loss, even if weight loss is a byproduct of fasting. There is a difference between intermittent fasting and a spiritual fast. One is to draw nearer to God, while the other is for weight loss, maintaining weight, or other health-related purposes. There is nothing wrong with intermittent fasting for weight loss. The problem is when you are doing a spiritual fast, and weight loss becomes your primary focus, then you will be missing out on the benefits of a spiritual fast. You will be more concerned with what you are not eating to lose weight than what you are seeking from God. Before I understood the purpose of fasting, I kept myself busy during my fasts.

For me, it was a way to keep my mind off food. And because I was not intentional, I did not see a breakthrough. It's important to know your purpose for your fast and be intentional about it. Expect that you will hear from the Lord. I mentioned that fasting is not a way to manipulate God. As embarrassed as I am to admit this, there was a fast I did that I now see was an attempt to twist God's arm on a situation. At the time, I had a neighbor who was heavily involved in witchcraft. She thrived on causing division amongst the neighbors, chaos, drama, control, and manipulation, among many other things. She latched on to anyone that gave her attention. Her phone calls and text messages to me averaged about 365 a month. When anyone tried to set healthy boundaries with her, she got ugly about it. I had pulled together a few of my Christian friends and suggested we do a group fast.

Many of us were burned out from this woman's deceptive behaviors, and we wanted her to move away. I was serious about this situation that I committed to completing a 7-day, liquid-only fast. With all of my heart, I believed that if I committed to doing this, then God would change the circumstance around and make her move out. Our group had already witnessed God move in other situations with regards to some of our previous fasts. We thought we had this one in the palm of our hands. Looking back now, I can almost see the Lord shaking His head, saying, my daughters, my daughters, I love the enthusiasm, but we must talk. As you can imagine, we did not get the results we had anticipated. At first, I felt discouraged because a 7-day liquid fast was a real sacrifice for me.

This reminds me of the book of Isaiah 58, where the Lord speaks about why He was not responding to their fast. More on that later in the chapter of Living a Fasted Life. Sometime later, the Lord revealed to me that my motives were not pure. He also reminded me that prayer and fasting go hand in hand. This fast, I did not spend much time in prayer. Our fasting did not come back to us empty-handed though. We continued to pray for this woman as well as the turmoil she was projecting on our neighbors. A change did take place, but because it was not the result we were looking for, we did not recognize the difference right away. This neighbor used to roam about being a busy body throughout our neighborhood from the time she woke up until she went to bed, and that came to a complete halt. Almost every morning, she was outside roaming about wearing her bathrobe and red lipstick. It was the same thing come evening, but evenings she was usually drunk.

The minute she heard one of us open our front door, she was not far behind chasing after us to share her latest gossip or drama. Not long after we finished the fast, we noticed she rarely came outside. In fact, she rarely opened the blinds to her windows anymore. The drama, gossip, and division in our neighborhood completely stopped. I eventually changed my begging of the Lord to make her move to a prayer for her salvation. Due to some unfortunate circumstances, she did eventually move away. God continues to show me how to have a powerful, fasted, and prayerful life. Something else important to note is that just because you do not see physical results immediately does not mean that God is not working in the spiritual realm on your behalf.

Biblical fasting is not valid without a sincere heart of obedience. It is not selfish and is not intended to glorify yourself. God sees right through hypocrisy and empty religious rituals. In Luke 18, Jesus points out how self-righteous the Pharisee was because he claimed to not be like all the others, and he fasted twice a week. Anyone who exalts himself above others will be humbled, just as the Bible says.

> [9] *To some who were confident of their own righteousness and looked down on everyone else, Jesus told this parable:* [10] *"Two men went up to the temple to pray, one a Pharisee and the other a tax collector.* [11] *The Pharisee stood by himself and prayed: 'God, I thank you that I am not like other people—robbers, evildoers, adulterers—or even like this tax collector.* [12] *I fast twice a week and give a tenth of all I get.'* [13] *"But the tax collector stood at a distance. He would not even look up to heaven, but beat his breast and said, 'God, have mercy on me, a sinner.'* [14] *"I tell you that this man, rather than the other, went home justified before God. For all those who exalt themselves will be humbled, and those who humble themselves will be exalted."* (Luke 18:9-14)

As you can see in Luke 18, Jesus points out that those who exalt themselves will be humbled, and those who humble themselves will be exalted. Jesus is more concerned with the condition of your heart than He is with religious doctrines. Do not fall into the trap of believing that you are a better Christian because you fast more than others. Throughout history, people have fasted with the wrong focus, seeking to earn God's favor or to prove their dedication to Him, but this is not what He is after. God delights in our obedience and our pursuit of intimacy with Him. This is so important to understand.

Biblical fasting is not a means for weight loss or a way to manipulate or twist God's arm. It is not without a sincere heart of obedience, nor does it make you a better Christian than those who do not fast.

Chapter Three

Different Types of Fasting

The Bible describes four major types of fasting, and the type of fast you choose is between you and God. You may be led to fast, and this is where the Holy Spirit will put it upon your heart to a particular fast. A church may call for a corporate fast, and this is when you as a church are in agreement with what type of fast and for how long. But you, yourself, may also choose to fast.

A Regular Fast

A regular fast is refraining from eating all food. Most people will drink water or juice during a regular fast. When Jesus fasted in the desert for 40 days, the Bible does not mention that He was thirsty. Matthew 4:1-2, *"Then Jesus was led up by the Spirit into the wilderness to be tempted by the devil. And when He had fasted forty days and forty nights, afterward He was hungry."* In this fast Jesus ate no food, but it does not state that He did not have water.

Absolute Fast

An absolute fast means absolutely no food or water. It is very important to understand that this type of fast should not be undertaken over three days and only then if you have a clear directive from the Lord. An absolute fast is also known as a supernatural fast, as in the case of Moses. (Deuteronomy 9:9)

Partial Fast

A partial fast can mean fasting certain meals of the day or refraining from certain foods. A few examples would be eating no meat, no sugar, or eating fruits and vegetables only. In Daniel 10:2-3, the Bible says that Daniel mourned for three weeks. He ate no choice food; no meat or wine touched his lips. And in Daniel 1:12, they ate only vegetables and water.

Corporate Fast

This is when a church or group feels God has called them to fast together for a certain period. Esther called for a corporate three-day fast. (Esther 4:16) Ezra declared a corporate fast and prayed for a safe journey. (Ezra 8:21)

Living a Fasted Lifestyle

The fasted lifestyle is about earnestly seeking intimacy with Jesus as we set aside our physical hunger for things. It is about prayer, fasting, serving, giving, and blessing others. Living a fasted lifestyle keeps you humble and helps you align your will with the perfect will of God. Isaiah 58 gives detailed instruction on living a fasted life, and I discuss more about this in the chapter, Living a Fasted Life.

Chapter Four

Duration of Fasting

The duration of your fast is entirely up to you and the leadership of the Holy Spirit. If you are going to do an Absolute Fast, I highly recommend not going more than three days and seek medical counsel first. Typically, a fast is for a specified length of time. However, there were occasions of fasting in the Bible that did not specify the length of their fast. A few examples taken from the Bible:

1. One Night Fast (Daniel 6:18)
2. One Day Fast (Judges 20:26, Nehemiah 9:1, 1 Samuel 7:6, 1 Samuel 1:12, Jeremiah 36.6)
3. Three Day Fast (Esther 4:16, Acts 9:9 Saul/Apostle Paul)
4. Seven Day Fast (1 Samuel 31:13, 2 Samuel 12:16, 1 Chronicles 10:12)
5. Fourteen Day Fast (Acts 27:33)
6. Twenty-One Day Fast (Daniel 10:3)
7. Forty Day Fast (Deuteronomy 9:9, 1 Kings 19:8, Matthew 4:2)
8. Unspecified Lengths (1 King 21:27, Ezra 8:23, Nehemiah 1:4, Acts 14:23)

As I began this new journey of incorporating fasting into my life, I could not help but wonder why people, including myself, were not fasting more often. If fasting and prayer are so life-changing and powerful, producing results while heightening our relationship with God, then why on earth are we as believers not fasting more often? This led me to seek the Lord about how to live a fasted lifestyle. I wanted this to be a big part of my life. But I did not know how to incorporate this because I did not want to abstain from food in a way that would be unhealthy for me. Yet, I did not want to take a chance on missing out on God's best for me. I also did not want fasting to become an idol in my life. While in prayer one day, I felt the Lord speaking to me about fasting certain meals of the day. Our fasts do not always have to be a full 3-day, 7-day, or 21-

day fast. We can fast breakfast for the week or fast lunch once a week. By fasting in this way, we can integrate fasting and prayer to become more prominent in our lives.

Rather than spending that time deciding what to eat, preparing your meal, and eating instead, use this time to prepare to hear from God. Whatever type of fast you choose, be intentional about it. Plan ahead and even pray about it before you commit. You don't claim a fast because you realized you forgot to eat breakfast one morning. That is not being intentional and most likely will not produce the same results. Try to incorporate a variety of fasting methods into your daily life. Many do not fast because they see it as hard work and fail to see that the benefits of fasting and prayer far outweigh the sacrifices.

Chapter Five

Incentives to Fasting

There are many incentives to biblical fasting. When combined with prayer, fasting can be a powerful and effective Christian discipline. I will discuss the benefits more in depth in the next chapters but here are a few. Fasting suppresses your flesh allowing you to be more sensitive to God. It strengthens your prayers and gets rid of unbelief. It releases breakthrough, deliverance, and healing. Fasting is one form of spiritual warfare. As noted earlier it is also one of the quickest ways to humble yourself. Maybe you are in a season where you are finding it hard to hear from God or you are feeling distant from Him.

Have you been praying for a breakthrough in an area of your life, but you haven't seen any changes? Maybe you need healing or answers to a health problem you or the doctors have not been able to figure out. Whether you are looking for a breakthrough, deliverance, to draw nearer to the Lord or even for repentance, fasting and prayer together is a step in the right direction. As we humble ourselves before God, He will respond.

1 Kings 21:27-29 says, *"So it was, when Ahab heard those words, that he tore his clothes and put sackcloth on his body, and fasted and lay in sackcloth, and went about mourning. And the word of the Lord came to Elijah the Tishbite, saying, "See how Ahab has humbled himself before Me? Because he has humbled himself before Me, I will not bring the calamity in his days. In the days of his son I will bring the calamity on his house."*

Fasting humbles the flesh and when it is done for that purpose, it pleases God. No matter how big or small your situation is, fasting and prayer produces victory. When you fast, there is renewed power because we are reminded that ultimately, we are dependent on God. You can experience many great things in life without fasting, but if you want to experience the blessings of a fasted lifestyle then fasting and prayer must become a part of your Christian walk.

When you think about how important food is to your well-being, abstaining from food for a certain time creates in you a dependence upon the Lord. When we humble ourselves before God, He draws nearer to us. Romans 12:2 says, *"Do not be conformed to this world, but be transformed by the renewal of your mind, that by testing you may discern what is the will of God, what is good and acceptable and perfect."* Prayer and fasting combined removes pride and arrogance allowing ourselves to humbly come before God. In return, this allows you to align your will with the perfect will of God. Don't you want to be in alignment with the perfect will of God?

Knowing God's will for your life and living out the will of God brings that perfect peace in your life and those around you. A peace that most of us spent years searching for. Many people spend a lot of time searching for their purpose or searching for something because they feel a void in their life. People join groups or cults because they want to feel like they are a part of something bigger. A lot of people will spend thousands of dollars on motivational coaches or business coaches. There is nothing wrong with having a coach or a mentor but what many fail to realize is that what they are searching for can be found in Jesus and His word. I have spent years and a lot of money on books and webinars on how to be successful and stay motivated. Little did I know at the time that God provides us with answers in His Word on how to live a prosperous life. For years I allowed my circumstances to define who I was. Today, I know who I am in Christ. I am a daughter of God Almighty and I know God has great plans for my life. A life with a purpose as opposed to just drifting through life.

God knew me and He knew you before you were in your mother's womb. Every single one of us was created on purpose by God and for a purpose. The self-doubt, fear of failure, and the worries of this world gradually diminished since I began to truly seek the Lord with all my heart. Fasting has played a big part in finding out what God's will is for my life. Fasting, prayer and spending time in God's Word has created in me a much greater desire to hold onto the personal relationship I have with Jesus. The Christian life is so much more than going to church on Sundays, bible study on Wednesdays and quick prayers before meals and bed.

It is so much bigger than that and until you experience the intimacy with Jesus you will always feel a void in your life. Another incentive to fasting and prayer that I do not really touch on in this book are the health benefits. You will be amazed at how better you feel after you have fasted for a period. Oftentimes,

I feel more energized after a fast. The incentives to fasting and prayer are abundant and far outweigh the sacrifice of giving up food.

Chapter Six

Fasting Suppresses Your Flesh

What does it mean to suppress the flesh and why should we? We are either being ruled by our flesh, which is our sin nature or we are being ruled by our spirit, which is the nature of God. In society today, we are surrounded by things that feed into our flesh. Whether it's the music we listen to, movies we watch, billboards, sexual immorality, idolatries (anything we put before God is an idol), and the list is endless. Even our emotions feed our flesh. Carnal or fleshly desires are anything that oppose the will of God or the Word of God. In order to take control of the flesh, we need to crucify it. The best way to crucify the flesh is to simply starve it out. Fasting is a powerful way that enables us to suppress our flesh. When you fast, you are telling your flesh no and saying yes to God. Your flesh is submitting itself to the Spirit. Spiritual power and wisdom are released as a result of submitting your flesh to the Spirit. The key is to desire more of God and less of yourself.

Jesus said to His disciples in the Garden of Gethsemane, *"The spirit indeed is willing, but the flesh is weak"* (Matt. 26:41). Fasting is not just about abstaining from food. It is an act of separating yourself exclusively to God. Before Jesus embarked on His earthly ministry, He went on a 40-day fast to subdue His flesh and strengthen the power of the Holy Spirit within Him. Just take a moment and ponder that. If Jesus Christ Himself fasted to suppress His flesh and strengthen the power of the Holy Spirit within Him, why would we think we can get away with doing anything less than that?

When we fast, we suppress our flesh and are able to come into a closer union with the Holy Spirit. One of the many blessings is that it opens our spiritual ears, so we are more open to hearing God. For example, when Daniel fasted for ten days from eating royal food and wine the King of Babylon offered to him, he gained heightened spiritual insight. How many times have you prayed and asked the Lord that He heightens your spiritual insight? This does not happen in the flesh, it is spiritual. The Bible says in Daniel 1:20 that at the end of the ten days, Daniel, Hananiah, Mishael, and Azariah were brought before the king, and none was found like them.

In all matters of wisdom and understanding, these men were found to be ten times better than all the magicians, astrologers, Chaldeans, soothsayers, and wise men. All four men were given knowledge, skill in all literature, and wisdom. And Daniel had understanding in all visions and dreams. Daniel was the only one in all the province who could interpret King Nebuchadnezzar's dreams and visions. Not even the wise men, Chaldeans, astrologers, magicians, and soothsayers were able to interpret the king's dreams. King Nebuchadnezzar had dreams that troubled him. One day he called in the magicians, astrologers, the sorcerers, and the Chaldeans to tell the king his dreams. Notice that the king wanted them to tell him his dream first. He did not share his dream with the Chaldeans first. The Chaldeans did not hesitate to ask the king to tell them his dream, at which point then they would give its interpretation. But the king refused and told them he wanted them to tell him of his dream first and then give its interpretation, or they would be cut to pieces, and their homes would become a heap of ash.

They again asked the king a second time to tell them his dream first, and they would give its interpretation. The king finally answered firmly and told them that if they did not make his dream known to him, there was only one decree for them. The king knew that if he first shared his dream with them, they would only be speaking lies and corrupt words. This is what witchcraft is all about. Astrology, soothsayers, magicians, and sorcerers are all witchcraft, from which God clearly tells us to stay away. There is knowledge that only the One true God can give us. The knowledge that comes from the enemy may have partial truth to it, but it will never beat the knowledge you get from the One true God. The Chaldeans answered and said no king has ever asked such things before and admitted that there is no way they could possibly know his dream. But, of course, they couldn't because the god they were serving was the god of this world.

The king then set out to kill all wise men of Babylon. When Daniel heard of this, he asked the king to give him some time. When King Nebuchadnezzar agreed to give Daniel time, Daniel sought God concerning this secret, and God spoke to him through a night vision. God gives wisdom to the wise and knowledge to those who have understanding. You may ask how does one become wise and have understanding so that God will provide us with wisdom and knowledge? Here are some of the most profound words in Scripture showing us that God is the source of all Godly knowledge and wisdom and that He wants to release this knowledge to us.

Proverbs 1:7 says, *"The fear of the Lord is the beginning of knowledge, but fools despise wisdom and instruction."* Ecclesiastes 7:19 says, *"Wisdom strengthens the wise more than ten rulers of the city."* James 1:5 says, *"If any of you lacks wisdom, let him ask of God, who gives to all liberally and without reproach, and it will be given to him."* Jeremiah 33:3 says, *"Call to Me, and I will answer you, and show you great and mighty things, which you do not know."* Daniel 2:28 says, *"But there is a God in heaven who reveals secrets...."*

God reveals deep and secret things to those who seek Him out. Nowhere in the Bible does it say that God works in mysterious ways. His Word, which is truth, is clear that He reveals secrets to those who seek Him out. Sure, there are certain things that we will not understand, but the phrase that God works in mysterious ways is taken out of context. Daniel told the king his dream and gave its interpretation.

Daniel also shared with the king that the secret that the king was asking cannot be known to the wise men, astrologers, magicians, soothsayers, but there is a God in heaven who reveals secrets. Notice that no amount of witchcraft, Tarot card reading, or Psychic abilities would have access to this kind of knowledge. I feel sorry for those who practice this type of thing because they believe they have some special powers or knowledge that the rest of us don't have. Little do they know that those who earnestly serve the One true God will always have more knowledge because we have the Holy Spirit living on the inside of us. Daniel was promoted and made ruler over the whole Province of Babylon. And the other three, Hananiah (Shadrach), Mishael (Meshach), and Azariah (Adeb-Nego), were set over the affairs of the Province of Babylon. These are not just stories about men that lived thousands of years ago. God's Word is for us today. When you fast, you crucify your flesh by fasting and nurture your spirit by prayer.

Your physical man decreases, so your spirit man can increase. You decrease, so God in you can increase. If you are not fasting, there is a certain part of God and victory that you are missing out on. Only when you crucify the flesh that blinds us can we see in the spiritual world. Think about that for a moment. When Jesus fasted, He was able to overcome every single temptation that the devil threw at Him. When Moses fasted for forty days and forty nights, he was given the Ten Commandments, which still affect us today. Fasting will affect you and your family for generations to come.

If fasting suppresses the flesh and inclines your ears to the voice of God, wouldn't this help you when you are seeking the Lord for direction in some area of your life?

Chapter Seven

Fasting Makes You Sensitive to God

The Bible says, *"So then faith comes by hearing, and hearing by the word of God."* (Romans 10:17) Faith does not come by fasting, but fasting can help us with being more sensitive to hearing the Word of God. Fasting allows us to enter an intense time of focus through prayer and seeking God for insight and wisdom. It is one of the most effective ways to experience increased sensitivity to hearing the voice of God. Maybe you've been seeking instruction from the Lord regarding a particular situation, but you are not hearing His voice. Perhaps you have been praying for a breakthrough in some area of your life but have not yet received the manifestation in the physical.

Maybe you have been feeling stuck in the same place, and you know there must be more, but you are not feeling led by the Lord on what direction to go. Sometimes, increasing our prayer time and doubling up on the Word of God will take care of it. However, if you need to hear divine direction from the Lord, fasting will suppress your flesh and open your spiritual ears to receive. It increases a more intimate relationship with God. I once heard someone describe intimacy as "into me." If you want to have an intimate relationship with someone, you need to draw into them.

The same is true with our Heavenly Father. It is difficult to hear the voice of the Lord when we are busying ourselves with our daily responsibilities or social activities. This is why fasting is so important. Fasting does not always have to be a certain number of days. Try fasting one meal for a day or for a certain amount of time. Whether it's a three-day, seven-day, twenty-one-day fast, or a one-meal fast, use that time to get away from all the busyness and all distractions. If you are at work, spend an hour in your car away from all distractions. Spend time in prayer, pull up the Bible app, meditate on a verse, and then wait on the Lord. If you are a stay-at-home parent and your only quiet time is when your little ones are napping, rather than busying yourself with everything you have on your to-do list before your little one wakes up, devote this time to the Lord. How many of you spend your lunch breaks checking social media? If you have time to watch television, scroll through social media, then you have time to go away to a quiet place and seek the Lord.

What worked for me was finding a space at home or outside where I was removed from all distractions. At this moment, my quiet space is a small corner in my bedroom. Other times I would take a weekend or a week to spend at my Aunt Mary's cabin in Northern Michigan. The little red cabin in the woods was a great place for me to get away from all distractions. There was no internet, and the cell phone service was minimal. By removing myself from all distractions, I was able to spend a lot of time in prayer, fasting, and meditating on God's Word. During this time, I also kept a journal because I had so many breakthrough moments that blew my mind.

When you make time for God, He answers. Years ago, when I committed to spending time alone with the Lord, it was a complete disaster. The first challenge for me was trying to figure out what part of the day worked best. In the past, my prayers were mostly at night while I was in bed for the evening. Which was useless because I was tired, and I only managed a few minutes in prayer and reading the Bible. A quick prayer before bed was fine, but I was trying to commit to spending more alone time with God in prayer, reading His Word, and waiting to hear from Him.

The next idea I had was to wake up early to spend at least an hour with Him. This proved to be a challenge because waking up earlier than 6:00 am was difficult for me, and when I did wake up early, the first thing I did was grab my coffee and check my phone, email, and social media. Before I knew it, hours had passed by, and it was time to get in the shower. Sometimes, I would even fall back to sleep. I realized doing my prayer time in bed would not work if my goal was to spend more time in prayer and in God's Word.

So, the next thing I did was create a prayer room in one of my walk-in closets. I had a nice walk-in closet in my bedroom. Giving this up and putting my clothes and my shoe collection in another bedroom was a big deal for me, but I was determined to find something that worked for me. I put a fresh coat of paint on the walls and put up a string of pastel lights. I had a small comfortable chair with a footrest, a small table with a lamp, a blanket, and candles. Now I was ready to make this commitment, but let me tell you that there would still be challenges to overcome even with this newly created space.

Before I went into my prayer room, I gathered everything I thought I might need, like my Bible, notebook, pen, and coffee. And I made the excuse that I may need my phone to look up the meaning of a verse or word. I would settle into my comfortable chair, ready to pray, but realized I should use the restroom before I start. After I got settled in again, I'd remember that I forgot to turn my phone on silent. But before I turned my phone to silent mode, I had to check my email quickly just in case an important message came through. After responding to a few emails, then I turned my phone to silent mode. By now I was sipping on lukewarm coffee, so I had to get back up to warm it in the microwave. While I would wait for my coffee to warm in the microwave, I figured it would be a good time to make a quick phone call or text. A half-hour later, I re-enter my prayer room. So far, I have taken care of the bathroom matters, checked my emails, made a quick call, switched my phone to silent mode, and warmed my coffee. After I settled in again, then I was hungry. I do not recall how many tries it took me before I learned how to go into my prayer room and focus on nothing else but my time with the Lord. It took many months before it became a habit to wake up before sunrise. When you make a commitment to spend a certain part of your day with the Lord, He looks forward to that time with you. You can always count on Him to show up for your scheduled meeting with Him. Will He be able to count on you to show up?

Many times, in Jesus's ministry, He sought solitude to pray. If Jesus made time to be alone to pray, we should realize the importance of removing ourselves from any distractions that would prevent us from hearing from our Heavenly Father. Making an honest effort to remove yourself from distractions will benefit you greatly, even if it's only for a short amount of time. During my times of solitude and fasting, my spiritual eyes and spiritual ears were more sensitive to hearing the voice of God. I have had people ask me if I really hear from God as well as people being skeptical of our ability to hear from Him.

The more time you spend with someone, you can recognize their voice on the phone even though you cannot see them. You know who is calling because you know their voice, right? It is no different with God. The more time you spend with Him you will begin to recognize His voice. Sometimes, it appears as an audible voice in your mind, a thought or a stirring in your spirit. Sometimes you will have this thought to look up a certain Bible passage, and it gives you an answer to something you were seeking God about.

I need to point out that sometimes I think I heard something from God but later found out it was not from Him. When I hear from God, I almost always write it in my journal and then will pray about it. If it is from God, you can usually find it in the Bible, or He will provide another way to confirm it was from Him. I remember one night I woke up in the middle of the night and had this thought of a friend I had not seen since High School. I thought it was strange that she came to mind and soon shrugged it off and tried to fall back to sleep. When I realized I was not going to be able to fall back to sleep, I prayed and asked the Lord if this was from Him.

I felt it was, and so I prayed for her. I was not given any specifics, so I just prayed for her safety and that God would comfort her. At the time, I had no idea what was going on in her life since I had not seen her since High School. Then, about five years later, I ran into her. I told her about the night God woke me up to pray for her in the middle of the night. I found out she was going through a divorce, and it was a tough time for her. It may be hard for some of you to believe that we can hear from the Lord, but I promise you, the more time you spend with Him, you too will become more sensitive to hearing His voice.

I want to share another story with you. One night I was praying for my significant other's safety because he was heading out of town late that evening after a long day of work during the winter months. During my prayer, I felt the Lord tell me he was meeting up with an old girlfriend. In fact, I had the feeling that at that very moment I was praying for him; he was with her, and they would share a kiss before the night was over. I had no idea who this ex could be because I did not know any of his previous girlfriends, except for the mother of his child. This is not the woman he was meeting up with though.

I had no reason to believe he would cheat on me. The thought never crossed my mind. This was a Friday night, and he would not be home until Sunday, which meant that I would have to wait a few days to ask him about it. Of course, I was wondering if this was from God or the enemy. As I said, I had no reason to believe he would cheat on me or be dishonest with me. Sunday arrived, and we decided to meet up at his place for lunch. I had no idea how I was going to bring this up to him without sounding like I was crazy. I did not arrive at his place angry or confrontational.

After we got the normal chit-chat out of the way, I asked him, if there was anything else he wanted to share with me about the weekend. His first response was no. So, I asked him, are you sure there is nothing else you should share with me about the weekend? This time he had a surprised look on his face, but again he said no. By this time, I knew by the look on his face that what the Lord shared with me was true. But I gave him another chance to come forward on his own. I was eager for him to be honest with me. Finally, I just came right out and asked him, did you meet up with anyone? His response was no. I told him I had something to share with him, and it may sound crazy. I admitted to him that I was nervous to say it out loud. By this point, I was no longer calm. In fact, I had butterflies in my stomach because I thought how crazy I would look if I was wrong.

I explained to him that when I was praying for him that Friday night, I felt the Lord share with me that he was having dinner with an ex that very moment, and by the end of the night, they would share a kiss. The look he gave me said it all. His face turned white as snow, and he looked shocked. I was shocked. He finally admitted that he met up with an ex-girlfriend for dinner, and they did share a kiss goodnight. The reason he gave me was that he never got closure when they broke up and this was a chance for him to get that. I think we were both surprised by this whole thing. Looking back now, God was trying to protect me. There were so many red flags and times that God spoke clearly to me about this relationship, yet I chose to ignore them all. Needless to say, this relationship eventually ended, but it was not without consequences. It's vital that we heed the warnings of our loving Heavenly Father.

I have a story to share about being sensitive to God's voice. I took my son to the park to play on the playground and hang out at the beach one day. While we were on the slide, I felt the Lord speak to me about a woman on the swing set. I thought He was asking me to go up to her and pray for her. I had never just gone up to a stranger and asked them if I could pray for them, so this was not something I wanted to do. Instead, I just said a quick prayer for her under my breath. But the feeling to go and pray for her was not going away. I fought this and told God there is no way I was going up to a stranger and asking her if I could pray for her. I got annoyed and decided to leave the playground and walk over to the beach area. Within a minute of me walking to the beach area, she showed up. I thought you have got to be kidding me. I let my son play in the water for a bit, but this lady was wading in the water not too far from my son. A bit miffed by it all, I told my son it was time to leave. We packed everything up, and as I was putting my son in his car seat in the back of the car, this lady started walking to her car. Guess where her car was parked? Right next to my car!

I got into the driver's seat, rolled up my windows, and told the Lord I am not going to do this. I regretted that later. The whole incident continued to bother me for the rest of the day. Later that evening, I was on the phone with a girlfriend and began to share my story. She asked me if this lady was on the swing at East Bay Park. I told her yes. Apparently, my friend had been at the same park just before me. The crazy part about this is my friend did not live in this city. She lived about an hour and a half away, and she rarely came to town. She responded the same way I did when God also put it upon her heart to go up to this woman and pray for her.

We both regretted not being obedient to what God was calling us to do, but we did pray for her together at that moment. I hesitated to share this story because I was not obedient to God, but I felt it was important to share because it shows that I was hearing from God because He spoke the same thing to a friend of mine. You can bet that after that experience, I will not be disobedient again when the Lord asks me to go up and pray for someone. The more time you spend in prayer and fasting, the more sensitive you will become to hearing the voice of the Lord.

Chapter Eight

Fasting Strengthens Our Prayers

The discipline of fasting and humbling ourselves before the Lord will draw us closer to Him, therefore strengthening our prayers. When you fast, you spend more time in prayer and seeking the Lord. It is during the times of drawing nearer to God that allow us to hear His voice. If you are using this time to renew your mind by reading and meditating on the Word of God, your heart begins to change. Your thoughts begin to change. You begin to change from the inside-out. It's truly a life changing transformation. You become more in alignment with what God's will is for your life. First and foremost, God's will for you is to have a personal relationship with you. He loves you so deeply!

If you read the book of Daniel, you will see how he strengthened his prayer life as he devoted himself to God. One example is in Chapter 9, where Daniel made a request by prayer and supplications with fasting. (Daniel 9:3) Reading further down in verse 20, it says that Gabriel had appeared to Daniel and told him that the command went out at the beginning of his supplications. It is not the fasting that determines whether God hears our prayers. God hears our prayers. But fasting changes our praying. When you fast, you are crucifying the flesh and giving heaven notice that you are serious.

This allows you to have a greater sense of focus and clarity in your prayers. It heightens the intensity of your prayers. There are stories of people who fasted and prayed and received divine intervention from God throughout the Bible. For example, in 1 Kings Chapter 21, Ahab, the king of Israel, received devastating news from Elijah. Because Ahab had done evil in the sight of the Lord, he was about to experience severe calamity. However, Ahab humbled himself and fasted. And because he humbled himself before the Lord, the Lord said He would not bring calamity in his days. Take a moment to read 1 Kings Chapter 21. You will see how God responded to a man that humbled himself before Him by spending time in fasting and prayer. Ordinary prayer requires faith, but fasting requires even more faith because you are completely dependent on God. God desires for us to be dependent on Him. It does not make you a weak person to be dependent on your Creator. Instead, this kind of dependency develops a close personal relationship with your Creator.

I understand all too well how being dependent on anyone, including God, may not come easy. We have all experienced someone letting us down when we let our guard down and allowed ourselves to be dependent on another person. People will let us down, but God will not. While prayer is the most talked-about Christian activity, it is the least activity practiced by most Christians besides fasting. Why is prayer so difficult? Besides the busy lifestyles we live and the many distractions, one of the reasons prayer is so difficult is because prayers sometimes lack results. How often have you prayed about something only to feel discouraged because you did not see any results?

If you want to see results in your prayer life, fasting must become a part of your Christian discipline. There have been times I had prayed about a certain outcome, but once I spent time in fasting and prayer over it, God gave me clarity. There are many reasons that the answers to our prayers are delayed or not answered in the way we want them answered. It may be that the timing is not right, and if that is the case, the Lord will give you the patience needed for His timing. Other times it turns out that what we think is best for us is not actually in our best interest. By adding fasting to your prayers, it reveals a greater determination. You are showing the Lord you are serious about this matter, and you need answers or direction.

When God observes His children forsaking themselves of all physical indulgences to draw nearer to Him, do you think He will not respond? Too often, people say a quick prayer, and that is the end of it. They do not turn to God's Word for answers or wait upon the Lord to hear His still, small voice. The truth is most people are so wrapped up in their own lives that many do not make time for God except for the occasional prayer or church on Sunday. Or worse, they only come to God when they are in a trial or a difficult season in their life.

People suddenly feel it's important to spend more time in prayer when things get difficult. Have you ever thought about how often, we as children of God, praise and give Him thanks? It amazes me how many people are desperate to hear from God during times of trouble but fail to give Him thanks when things are going well. Of course, it is important to praise God always. There are answers to almost every situation in the Bible. But if you don't read the

Bible faithfully, how will you know how God feels about a certain topic or situation?

It was not too many years ago that I thought the Bible was boring to read. I thought the stories in the Bible had nothing to do with us today. Now I look forward to reading the Bible. One example of how some people may not feel that the Bible pertains to us today is on the subject of healing. Some do not believe that God is still in the healing business. But, if God is the same today, yesterday, and tomorrow and His Word clearly states that we were healed by the stripes of Jesus, then why would this promise not apply to us today? God desires that we all are in good health, and He wants the sick to be healed.

Did you know the Bible covers the topic of immigration? Our country today is divided on immigration issues. The Bible has plenty of stories that cover the need to enter a country legally. Even in the Bible days, people had to follow proper protocol to enter a country legally, whether it was passing through, seeking a new place to live, or seeking protection.

The Bible also says that God reveals hidden things and things to come. Daniel 2:22 says, *"He reveals deep and secret things; He knows what is in the darkness, And light dwells with Him."* Have you ever had that gut feeling that something was off? That gut feeling can otherwise be described as the Holy Spirit speaking to you or giving you a warning. For example, when you have a gut feeling that you should not go somewhere, that may be the Holy Spirit warning you there is danger ahead. Maybe a friend you have not seen in years is suddenly coming to your mind. If the thought is persistent, it may be the Holy Spirit telling you to pray for that person or call them. Daniel fasted and prayed, and God revealed things to him that not even the magicians, sorcerers, or even all the wise men knew. There is plenty of proof in the Bible that fasting strengthens our prayers.

Fasting creates a new level of urgency for prayer and brings a greater sense of clarity. The more time you spend praying, fasting, and reading the Bible, you will notice a shift in your prayers. There have been several times when I'm praying out loud, whether by myself or in a group, and the words that come out, I knew, were not words that I would have typically spoken on my own. Sometimes when I go into prayer, I will already have something on my mind that I want to pray about. But something shifts in me, and before I know it, my prayer is bold, spoken with confidence, and it flows seamlessly. I keep a journal of some of my prayers, answered prayers as well as revelations I receive as I'm reading the Bible. When I look back at some of those journals, I am amazed at what I wrote. Those are not words or revelations I could have come up with on my own. Instead, the Holy Spirit gave me supernatural revelation on something that my carnal mind could not see on its own.

One of the best parts of going back and reading journals I had written earlier is when it's something I needed to hear that day. Of course, I have those thoughts sometimes like, wow, I wrote that? My gosh, I'm good, but then I'm quickly reminded that it was God who showed me that. Sometimes when I am praying, I will sense the presence of the Holy Spirit so strongly that it brings me to tears. And sometimes, it's a full-blown, uncontrollable cry. I don't necessarily understand that, but it does happen to me a lot.

One day a friend and I decided at the last minute to pray in the early morning before we both headed out for the day. It was already a busy morning for me, even before we met to pray at 8:00 am. I had to leave by 8:10 am, so when she did come over for prayer, I figured it would be a quick prayer. I was praying, and out of the blue, tears just started rolling down my cheeks. I tried desperately to hold them back so my mascara would not run all over, but suddenly I was crying. I was not sad, and we were not praying over something sad, but the presence of the Holy Spirit in my home that morning was so incredibly intense.

Matthew 18:20 says, *"For where two or three are gathered together in my name, I am in the midst of them."* Because I was heading to an appointment, I had to touch up my makeup quickly and rush out the door. As I was driving to my appointment, all I could think about was where on earth did that come from? I think the more time we spend with Jesus, we become more aware of His presence. I encourage you today that if you are interested in strengthening your prayer life, then make the commitment to add fasting and meditating on God's Word. When you incorporate Scripture into your prayers, it becomes even more powerful because you speak God's living Word into your prayer.

When I am feeling down about something or concerned about a situation, I will look up Scripture related to my situation. And rather than just read it I will personalize it and speak it aloud. Because of the power of God's Word, almost always, I feel immediate peace. I won't stop until I have peace. So, the next time you are concerned about something, look up passages in the Bible that relate to your situation. When you declare God's promises, you are declaring that God is not the problem. The power of darkness is the one that is holding back the blessing.

When you pray, you pray to bring heaven down to earth. More often than not, the reason prayers go unanswered is due to the way people are praying. When you are begging and pleading with God, you negate everything that Jesus did on the cross. Under the new covenant, everything changed because of what Jesus did on the cross for us. If you are not studying the Bible, you will not have an understanding of what God's promises are for you, nor will you understand the authority we have in Christ. Therefore, how can you declare God's promises over your life? You need to partner with God and boldly declare His promises for you.

Almost every morning, I pray over my son. I declare God's promises over him. One morning I skipped the morning prayer and figured I would do it in the afternoon at some point. After my son got out of work that day, he called me and asked me if I forgot to pray for him. He shared with me that he had the worst day and shared some of the situations that took place that day. My heart broke. All day I had this feeling that I needed to stop what I was doing and pray for my son, but I ignored the promptings.

My prayer life is not perfect, but I do my best to pray often. There are times I wondered if my prayers make a difference in my son's life, my life, or my family's. After my son shared with me that he can tell when I have prayed for him and don't, I knew at that moment that my prayers do make a difference. My son and I laughed about this for days later because it confirmed to both of us that our prayers matter and are powerful. There have also been times that my son has also texted me during the day to ask me if I had just prayed for him because something happened at that moment that He knew was from God.

In the past, my prayer life was what I would call a basic prayer life. But the more time I spent fasting, my prayer life strengthened. I learned the importance of proclaiming God's Word and His promises over my life and my family's. The more time you spend in fasting and prayer, you too will learn how to strengthen your prayer life. You will learn how to declare God's promises over yourself, your family, finances, career, relationships, and health. And more importantly, your love for God will strengthen. Your desire to know and understand Him, will deepen.

Chapter Nine

Fasting Gets Rid of Unbelief

According to biblestudytools.com, the word unbelief in the King James Version represents two Greek words, apeitheia, "disobedience" (only in Romans 11:30,32; Hebrews 4:6,11), and apistia, "distrust," the antithesis to "faith." Unbelief, according to dictionary.com, is "the state or quality of not believing; incredulity or skepticism, especially in matters of doctrine or religious faith." Thus, unbelief is the absence or rejection of belief. We have been taught to live our lives based on our five senses. What we can see, smell, hear, feel, and taste. If we can test it with our five senses in our carnal minds, it's easier for us to believe.

But it is hard for us to believe in something that we cannot test with our five senses. According to Hebrews 11:1, *"Now faith is the substance of things hoped for, the evidence of things not seen."* And in Romans 10:17, *"So then faith comes by hearing, and hearing by the word of God."* One of my favorite teachers once said that most people do not let the Bible get in the way of their beliefs. It's true because most people are more moved by their circumstances than they are by the Word of God. This is an area I struggled with most of my life and still do today at times. Every day I must remind myself that God is bigger than my circumstances.

You can believe but still struggle with unbelief. Faith can be voided by unbelief. Unbelief limits how much of the power of God you can see in your life. If Jesus says that all things are possible to him who believes, then we should all be doing all we can to help with our unbelief. Fasting ignites the faith in us far quicker than any other process, besides reading the Bible. It is our very weakness through fasting that builds up faith. Paul said in 2 Corinthians 12:10, *"...for when I am weak, then I am strong."* Matthew 17:17-21 says, *Then Jesus answered and said, "O faithless and perverse generation, how long shall I be with you? How long shall I bear with you? Bring him here to Me." And Jesus rebuked the demon, and it came out of him; and the child was cured from that very hour. "Then the disciples came to Jesus privately and said, "Why could we not cast it out?" So, Jesus said to them, "Because of your unbelief; for assuredly, I say to you, if you have faith as a mustard seed, you will say to this mountain, 'Move from here to there,' and it will move; and nothing will be impossible for you. However, this kind does not go out except by prayer and fasting."*

Notice that Jesus said, "O faithless and perverse generation." It was their lack of faith that kept them from curing the boy of his sickness. And later, Jesus answered them and said, it's because of your unbelief. A lot of people take these verses to mean that demons can only be cast out by fasting. In this case, the demon is the illness. However, it is not the prayer and fasting that drive the demons out. No, what Jesus was saying is that fasting and prayer is the only way of casting out this type of unbelief. Unbelief is serious. It can keep people in bondage. Unbelief can keep us from receiving healing.

Jesus said that if you want to have more faith, you must put action to your faith. You have to do something. You don't get more faith by sitting around. You get more faith by pressing into God. If you lack faith and struggle with unbelief, it is because you have not been spending enough time in fasting, prayer and in His Word. I hear people say that they wish they had more faith or that their faith is not that strong. We were all given the same amount of faith but it's up to you to learn how to activate your faith. Faith comes by hearing and hearing the Word of God.

Unbelief can limit what God can do in your life and it can hold you back from receiving your breakthrough or direction for your life. Too often, people think that everything that happens in their life must be because God wanted it to happen. This is not true. I have had people tell me that the reason they are going through something terrible is because God must be testing them or trying to teach them something. God's sovereignty is so often misunderstood. Not everything we go through is because God wanted us to go through it.

Yes, God is sovereign but the very definition of sovereign means having supreme rank. That does not mean God controls everything. It does not mean that His will always come to pass. The Bible says that it is God's will that none shall perish, but that all should come to repentance. Scripture tells us that many will not make it. Many does not mean some, it means the majority. Some of the teachings on the sovereignty of God suggests that Jesus is in the driver's seat while we sit in the passenger seat. However, Scripture says, that we are in the driver seat because God gave us authority. Scripture also teaches us that we are supposed to be taking directions from the Lord. God gave man authority over his own life, but in order to succeed, he must receive direction from the Lord.

Some people don't want to be saved and accept Jesus Christ as their Lord and Savior. God does not force us to accept Him. Nowhere in the Bible does God tell us to sit back while He does all the work. Our words, thoughts, actions, beliefs, and unbelief play a part in the outcome of every situation. This may be hard for some to understand. But it all goes back to why God created us. God created us to have an intimate relationship with Him.

Referring to Matthew chapter 17, there is a difference between unbelief because of the lack of knowledge and understanding and the unbelief that comes from our carnal minds. The disciples, in this case, were being dominated by their natural senses rather than by God's supernatural Word. Jesus said that overcoming this unbelief brought on by the disciples' natural senses is to deny our senses through prayer and fasting. Remember I said in an earlier chapter that fasting suppresses the flesh. This is exactly what Jesus was saying to His disciples.

Please understand this, fasting is not just a religious doctrine. Fasting will change your life. We all struggle with unbelief at some point. Our natural senses tend to get in the way of our faith. Faith is the substance of things hoped for, not yet seen. Meaning not yet seen in the physical realm. It was not that the disciples did not believe in God's power to cure this boy, but they were more sensitive to what they saw. Jesus said in Matthew 17:20, if you have faith as a mustard seed, you can move mountains, and nothing will be impossible for you.

It is easy to mistake thc difference between believing that God can do something and believing only by what you see. Your unbelief will hinder your faith and your prayer life. Reading the Bible is necessary. There is no short cut to quickening your faith. If you want to move those mountains, then pray and fast. Faith and fasting go together! Just like faith and reading God's Word go together. If you are going to address the mountains in your life, you must first start at the root of that mountain. It is not enough to look at the external, visible mountain.

Much of what we experience on the outside is a result of what is rooted on the inside of us. I believe that much of our sickness and depression today stems from what we allow our eyes to see and our ears to hear. I disconnected cable years ago because much of what is on TV, including the commercials, were not producing good fruit in my life. The mainstream media, movies, and commercials are packed full of negative information. In a lot of cases, it is damaging to our minds and our health. How many commercials are there today that have to do with medications for depression, insomnia, arthritis, thyroid disease? It's on TV, the radio, billboards, and social media ads.

When your mind is constantly being bombarded with messages about sickness or ailments, it's easy to think upon those very things. The advertising companies understand the power behind their ads, and that is why they spend billions on advertisements annually. If you do not believe that these ads hold no power over your thoughts, think about the times you have watched a commercial with your favorite food or drink. Your mouth begins to water just thinking about it. Or you see a commercial for the latest diet fad, and the next day you're posting all over social media that it's Day 1 of your weight loss journey.

Yet God's Word tells us to meditate on the things that are pure, true, and lovely. Every instruction in the Bible has a purpose. God's Word was not written apathetically. God means what He says and says what He means. In my opinion, other causes for much of our sickness stems from unforgiveness, bitterness in our hearts, and fear. A bitter heart is a result of a hardened heart, and fear does not come from God. Have you ever thought about how deeply fear affects your body and emotions? Going through a pandemic for the first time in my life, I admit there was some fear in the beginning. But I quickly rejected that fear and replaced it with what God's Word says.

We prayed over our home and each other. We proclaimed Psalm 91 and other Scripture over ourselves and our home. I know what fear does to me, and times in the past, I have felt paralyzed by fear. I refused to let the enemy have this hold in my life or my son's. I knew if we allowed this fear to take hold of our hearts and minds, there was a good chance it would lower our immune system due to the stress that fear causes on our bodies. Sickness does not come from God. I know the power of God's spoken Words, so I chose to speak life, which is God's Word, rather than death into our lives and our home. Obviously, there are many other reasons for sickness and diseases, and I am not suggesting that every sickness is the person's fault. We live in a fallen world, and we will experience sickness, death, loss, and grief.

Many of us are trying to move the mountains that are seen without addressing that which is not seen. Sometimes, the root cause can be traced back to what we allow into our minds. If you ask the Lord what the root cause is, He will reveal it to you. The Bible says that when we diligently seek Him, we will find Him. When we knock, the door will be opened.

One of the unbelief strongholds in my life was believing that God would forgive me of some of the sins I have committed. Some were so great that for years I could not forgive myself. And I believed that if I had a hard time forgiving myself, then surely my Heavenly Daddy would have a hard time forgiving me. That is a clear indication that I hardly knew the heart of our all-loving God. I will never forget two moments I had while at church many years ago. I remember the pews I was sitting in each time and who was next to me. It was during worship, and I suddenly felt this rush of love overcome me. I began to cry and was not able to stop. The crying was not like something I had experienced before. It was not loud enough for the entire church to hear me the first time this happened, but those standing next to me knew. They were good friends of mine, and they knew why I was crying. However, I was still embarrassed because I don't like to cry in front of others.

There was a decision I made many years before that broke my heart and would affect the rest of my life. I knew it was wrong, I knew it was not part of God's will, but I was very selfish at the time. Over the years, I had repented and asked God for forgiveness. A part of me believed that God had forgiven me, but I learned that day at church that I had not forgiven myself. God's love had washed over me, and I knew at that moment that God had forgiven me, and I had to forgive myself. But the struggle was not over yet.

Not long after when I was back at church, and while we were singing the song Draw Me Close, I began to cry again. This time it was worse than the first time. I do believe this time, the entire church heard me. God was showering me with His love and letting me know it was time to forgive myself. My job now was to rebuke the lies of the enemy when he tried to convince me otherwise. To this day, the enemy tries to steal my joy and peace regarding past sins, but I am more mature now in knowing who I am in Christ. It is not likely we will forget our mistakes, but we sure can learn from them. When God forgives us, He remembers the sin no more, and He will not bring it up again.

Unbelief is believing something contrary to God's Word. If you have ever known that kind of unbelief, you understand how damaging it can be. It can affect many decisions you will make in your lifetime. It can hinder your prayers. You may struggle with unbelief in several areas. You may question whether you are really born again. Maybe you struggle with unbelief in whether you will be healed from a sickness or disease. Maybe your unbelief lies in whether God hears your prayers or wants to see you succeed. Whatever it is, I promise you that if you lay it all at the feet of Jesus, He will guide you through it. I suggest writing out the areas where you struggle with unbelief, then take it all to God. Pray about it; ask Him to show you what He says about it. Look up Bible verses about those topics and ask the Lord to give you understanding.

Be sure to meditate on the verses that are specific to what you are seeking the Lord for. I will sometimes write them down on a sticky note or in the notes on my phone and ponder them throughout the day. I have gone as far as setting a reminder on my phone every hour to look at that verse or verses. When God gives you an understanding of His Word, it changes your thoughts and your beliefs. This is valuable when you find yourself falling back to old thinking habits. For example, the minute I start feeling unworthy, I remind myself what God's Word says, and I speak those Scripture verses aloud.

Renewing your mind night and day along with fasting will help you to remove any unbelief you may struggle with. Take God's promises from the Bible and personalize them to your situation. For example, you can personalize Deuteronomy 28:8, The Lord will command the blessing on me in my storehouses and in all to which I set my hand to, He will bless. Personalize Isaiah 54:14, In righteousness I shall be established; I shall be far from oppression, for I shall not fear; and terror shall not come near me.

Chapter Ten

Fasting Releases Supernatural Protection of God

I feel it's important to point out again it is not the fasting itself that releases the supernatural protection of God. It is the act of humbling ourselves before the Lord. The Bible is filled with real life stories of God's people fasting and praying for His protection. Ezra was leading a crew that included families with little ones and their possessions from the river of Ahava to Jerusalem, and he knew the dangers that lay ahead. Ezra was faced with a decision to either rely on the king's soldiers and horsemen to protect them or rely on God. He did not want to rely on the king because he had spoken to the king before that the hand of God is upon all those for good who seek Him, and the power and wrath are on those who forsake Him.

He could have chosen the carnal path of relying on the king's soldiers, but he chose the spiritual way, which was to rely on God. Ezra proclaimed a fast so that they may humble themselves before God and seek from Him protection from the enemy and for direction. When they departed, the hand of God was upon them, and God delivered them from the hand of the enemy and the ambush that was along the road. (Ezra 8:21-13) The power of fasting and prayer bound every danger that lay ahead of them and allowed them to pass through in peace and security without losing a single member of their crew.

In 2 Chronicles 20:15, Jehoshaphat proclaimed a fast for protection from the people that were on their way to battle against Jehoshaphat. In verse 15, the Lord answered and said, *"Do not be afraid nor dismayed because of this great multitude, for the battle is not yours, but God's."* Another example is in the book of Esther. If you have not read the book of Esther, I recommend you do. At least read Chapters 3-7 right now. This is one of my favorite stories in the Bible because it goes to show that what the enemy meant for harm, God will and does turn it around for the good of those who love Him. Haman had just been promoted, and all the servants within the king's gate were to bow and pay homage to Haman.

But Mordecai, a Jew, would not bow to Haman. Therefore, Haman ordered a decree to exterminate Mordecai and all Jews who were throughout the whole kingdom of Ahasuerus. Esther and Mordecai were not about to accept this kind of injustice. They did not sit back passively and accept their fate by saying something stupid like I guess this is just my lot in life, or this must be part of God's plan. No, instead, they understood the power of prayer and fasting. They understood that when you fast and pray, things shift around in the atmosphere. Fasting and prayer bring about supernatural intervention, supernatural breakthrough, and supernatural protection.

Esther realized prayer alone was not enough in this situation. So, she called for a corporate 3-night fast of no food or water in order to defeat their enemies. They did this for divine intervention and for overcoming the decree by humbling themselves through prayer and fasting. In return, God responded, and the decree that Haman ordered backfired on him. One of my favorite parts of this story was when the king asked Haman what shall be done for the man whom the king delights to honor? See, King Ahasuerus had just found out that Mordecai was the one that informed him of the two eunuchs that wanted to kill him, which ultimately saved his life. Because of that the king wanted to recognize the man that helped in saving his life.

The king was referring to Mordecai, but Haman thought the king was talking about him when he asked him what should be done for the man whom the king delights to honor. Because he thought the king was talking about him, he suggested in verse 7, *"And Haman answered the king, "For the man whom the king delights to honor, let a royal robe be brought which the king has worn, and a horse on which the king has ridden, which has a royal crest placed on its head."* (Esther 6:6-8).

The king was talking about Mordecai, the very man who Haman wanted to hang and even made a gallows pole to hang him on. One of my favorite parts of this chapter is that the king ordered Haman to do exactly what Haman suggested. But, instead, it would not be Haman wearing the royal robe and riding the horse and wearing a crest on his head. No, it would all be Mordecai. So, Haman led Mordecai on horseback throughout the city square. Afterward, Haman went back to his house, mourning with his head covered. I imagine he was furious and despised Mordecai even more now. Another interesting fact is that Haman was killed the same way he was planning to have Mordecai killed.

The very day that the enemies of the Jews had hoped to overpower them, the opposite occurred. Instead, the Jews defeated all of their enemies. Mordecai ended up being promoted and was second to the king. What the enemy intended for evil; God turned it around. Everything Haman plotted against Mordecai and the Jews backfired on him. Haman was hung on the very gallows pole he had made to hang Mordecai on. The plot against God's people was turned into glorious success for the Jews. The power of Satan invoked by Haman backfired on him, while the power of the Holy Spirit invoked by Ester provided the absolute victory.

Can you imagine what would happen if believers today came together and proclaimed a fast over their city or better yet, for their state? I get so frustrated when I see churches today sending out mass emails or posting on social media to pray for something. I personally feel a corporate fast would hold a lot more power in releasing supernatural intervention. It's a shame that our churches are not stepping up to the plate to lead believers into corporate fasting. When we come together as a group, humbling ourselves before the Lord, things shift around in the atmosphere. Prayers are answered, miracles happen, strategies and hidden secrets are revealed. God turns things around for good for those who love Him and what the enemy meant for harm, backfires.

Many years ago, shortly after I re-dedicated my life to Christ, which was right around the time my son was born, I was up against a very draining spiritual battle. From the outside looking in, it would seem the battle was more in the physical realm than the spiritual realm. But I knew enough to understand this was the enemy coming up against me using some of my closest friends. A good friend of mine was fighting me for something that required us to go to court. This is not something that he would have done on his own. I have known this man for many years, and he would never have treated me this way had he not been influenced by someone with impure motives. Not only was this close friend turning on me, but my best friend of many years joined in.

Another friend also joined them. Previously, this friend had gone out of her way to write me letters expressing how much she looked up to me, yet here she was joining them. Three people that I thought were my friends and people I could count on turned on me. This was by far one of the hardest and most hurtful times in my life. The depth of the betrayal caused my heart to want to hate these people.

I knew the dangers of hate and knew better not to let this fester in my heart, so I cried out to God a lot during this time. I prayed that He would help me overcome this hate that was starting to brew within me. It was during one of my prayer times that the Lord directed me to Ephesians 6:10. I read this chapter every day and some days several times a day. I depended on these promises. Ephesians 6:10-17 says,

[10]Finally, be strong in the Lord and in his mighty power. [11]Put on the full armor of God so that you can take your stand against the devil's schemes. [12]For our struggle is not against flesh and blood, but against the rulers, against the authorities, against the powers of this dark world and against the spiritual forces of evil in the heavenly realms. [13]Therefore put on the full armor of God, so that when the day of evil comes, you may be able to stand your ground, and after you have done everything, to stand. [14]Stand firm then, with the belt of truth buckled around your waist, with the breastplate of righteousness in place, [15]and with your feet fitted with the readiness that comes from the gospel of peace. [16]In addition to all this, take up the shield of faith, with which you can extinguish all the flaming arrows of the evil one. [17]Take the helmet of salvation and the sword of the Spirit, which is the word of God.

While I was at a women's church service, one night, God spoke to me about my situation. We were all praying in the Spirit that night, and the leaders were calling people upfront to speak a word to them or pray over them. I had no idea they would be calling my name. I was quite content sitting in the very back row, minding my own business. Then, out of the blue, one of the leaders said, "Jen, are you ready?" This surprised me because the leaders that night did not know me, let alone my name. We had never met before that night. Reluctantly, I went up front, and I will never forget what the lady said to me.

She said, and I quote this because I wrote it down in my journal that night, "There is a lot of deception. Not because of you, but it's brought on by other people coming against you. God is asking, are you willing to forgive them?" Needless to say, I was taken aback by the question of me forgiving them. I was even miffed by it. Especially when God knew they had conspired against me to hurt me. However, I remembered my plea to God to help me overcome this hate that was starting to take hold of my heart. At that moment, I agreed to forgive them. I began to pray for every single one of them, and the Lord softened my heart towards all of them. It did not take long before I began to feel love in my heart for each one of them again. I realized that the main person who started this plot against me was very insecure about my friendship and my role with the others involved.

None of this had anything to do with me personally. The enemy brought this on, and each one of the people that came up against me had their own struggles and insecurities. All of them had also recently witnessed a change in me since I re-dedicated my life to Christ, and I think that change scared them. My best friend did admit that she had noticed a big change in me, but she suggested it was for the worse. I knew this was not true because several people had told me that the change in me was amazing. A major change was that I was no longer participating in gossip, and this friend loved to gossip and make judgements about others.

The only countermeasure I could come up with was to hand it all over to God and let Him handle it for me. I prayed for each of them and wholeheartedly trusted that God had me covered. When it was time for our court date, all I can say is that my God showed up in the courtroom. I was nervous yet calm. The lies that were spoken against me were quickly shut down when I was able to provide solid proof that they were lying. My organizational skills came in handy. The concepts that I learned from being a real estate agent to have everything in writing and my accounting background to keep a record of all accounting was extremely useful. Many years later, I ran into my old best friend, and she sincerely apologized for the way she betrayed me.

I want to share another story where God protected me and showed up in the courtroom once again. A while back, I took on a side job working for an acquaintance. The guy I was working for owned quite a few rental properties and offered me a discounted rate on one of his rentals since I was doing some work for him. It was agreed upon upfront that should we part ways, then the rental rate would go back to full rate immediately. I was supposed to be moved into one of his rental's Memorial weekend, but due to tenant issues, I was not able to move in until Mid-June.

The first red flag to not move into one of his rentals should have been when he tried to force me to pay rent when I had not even moved in yet. Which was no fault of my own. Shortly after I moved in, a lot of things went wrong. The water heater broke and leaked water all over. Not too long after, I found out there was water under the floors, and this was due to the shower leaking. The flooring was damaged and began to bubble. There was water in the walls in the bathroom, deadly black mold in the laundry room, electrical issues, poor insulation, and much more. This would also explain why I was sick so much. I got sick three times in three months and I rarely catch a cold. At this time, I was paying a high premium for a home that was considered uninhabitable. It would be a few short months before I quit my job with this person. After I quit, he immediately sent out a letter that my rent had increased. He also refused to pay me my last paycheck.

After I received the letter for a rent increase, I suggested that he give me a reduction in rent due to the place not being habitable. He refused, and I stopped paying rent. Before I knew it, there was an eviction in process, and he was trying to convince me to sign a pocket judgment. Again, I refused to pay him anything because he did not pay me my last paycheck, and the home was full of deadly black mold and was considered uninhabitable. I admit that when I found out we were going to court over this, I was nervous. I had never been to court over something like this, and the thought of a judgment on my record had me shaking in my boots.

Our First Day in Court.

As weird as it sounds, the plaintiff and I sat together in the courtroom. He asked me if I wanted to go into another room to see if we could mediate this ourselves. I explained to him that I did not see the purpose if he was not willing to compromise at all, not to mention we were the first case to go in front of the Judge that morning. Reluctantly, I finally agreed to discuss this further with him in one of the mediation rooms. I had no idea at this moment this would be to my advantage. We talked, and just as I suspected, he refused to compromise. I told him once the Judge reviewed my records, he would surely agree with me in that the home was uninhabitable. He said to me, "We'll see about that." We walked back into the courtroom, and as I suspected, we were now going to be the last case in front of the Judge. This worked to my advantage because I was able to hear all the cases before me. By hearing all the other rental cases before me, I learned that I would not be required to sign a consent judgment, but instead, I could inform the Judge that I wanted to seek legal counsel. I did not think to hire an attorney until I listened to the cases that were ahead of mine.

Doing this would mean the Judge would have to set another court date in the future. As I told the Judge I would like to seek legal counsel, he just smiled at me and said, "Well, obviously, you now know that is your right, and I have to grant that." We had another court date set, and, in the meantime, I obtained a lawyer. I hired Craig Elhart in Traverse City, MI. My family and I absolutely adore Craig and we have a great deal of respect for him. He offered to take my case at no cost! This was a huge blessing and definitely a God thing.

I handed over this massive file to my attorney, Craig Elhart. I had records of every single email between this individual and myself, every text, phone call log, and all the requests for repairs that I submitted. I had videos of the water under the floor, water leaking in the walls, and the leaking water heater. Also in my possession were mold inspection reports from two different companies proving that there was deadly black mold in the home. I had a letter from my son's doctor stating his concern with my son's excessive use of the inhalers. I did not seek this letter out from my son's doctor. He actually called me one day and requested an immediate appointment to see my son. The doctor was concerned with my son's excessive use of the inhaler and I explained to him that it was most likely due to the black mold in the home we were renting. I handed this file over to my attorney, and Craig took it from there. I rarely spoke to Craig and honestly had no idea what was going on. I trusted him, and I trusted God. I understand that some people don't trust lawyers, but I trusted Craig. I was confident that Craig had my back and was there to protect me.

Our 2nd Time in The Courtroom.

Up until our second court date, my opposing party was still trying to bully me into signing a judgment. I refused every single time. In the meantime, my attorney had filed a counter judgment. I walked into the courtroom with my attorney, and the other party seemed quite surprised to see an attorney at my side. He was not used to his tenants fighting back. Because he owned a lot of rental properties, he spent a lot of time in the court room. At our hearing, the Judge told us he could not hear our case that day because his rentals are in a Property Management company. Therefore, it is mandatory that he have an attorney present. So, the Judge had no choice but to set another court date.

Again, to my advantage, because during this time, I was instructed by Craig Elhart not to make any rental payments. My attorney asked me what I wanted out of all of this. I told him all I was looking for was to have the rent reduced by half. He suggested I pay him nothing after he reviewed all of the evidence. So, Craig filed for a countersuit as well as constructive eviction. A few days before our next court date, this individual was now attempting to negotiate something with me. Had he begun with this proposal; we would never have gone to court in the first place. But at this point, Craig is now telling me not to pay this man a penny.

I thought I would play along, though, just to see where he was at. I told him if he wants to cut the rent in half, I may consider it. He still refused, and by this time, I had already found a condo to buy. The new amount he was suing me for had doubled. To make things worse, after I moved out, he sent me an itemized list of damages for a total of $3100. On this itemized list, he was trying to charge me for nail holes. Are you kidding me? After all the cleaning and painting I did to that place? Not to mention the few hundred I spent on yard clean up. He began harassing me and trying to intimidate me by phone calls, emails, and showing up at my place of work. I sent him a letter back stating I refused to pay any of it. A few days before our next court date, I received a proposal from him.

He proposed that I pay him half of what he was suing me for, and it was to be paid in 60 days. Otherwise, they would go for the full amount. I refused his proposal. In the meantime, I spent much time in prayer. I read Scripture on God in the courtroom and on God's vengeance. Anytime I began to feel anxious about this situation, I handed it over to God, and peace immediately flooded me. I barely thought about our upcoming jury trial. I found out that the other individual was a total wreck. He had quit all fun activities and told his friends he would not be joining them on their weekly meetups until this was over. Apparently, he was really stressed out over this situation.

Our 3rd Time in The Courtroom.

This court date was to set our jury trial panel. About an hour before our court appearance, I received a call from my attorney. Craig told me that the opposing attorney had just called him, and they wanted to know if I'd like to meet to see if we can come to some agreement. I said, "At this point, the only way I will meet is if he wants to drop his case, and then I will drop mine, otherwise NO!" He said, "Yeah, I don't think that's why he wants to meet." I said, "Well, tell him no and that I will see him at trial in an hour." This was his last-ditch effort to get some money out of me. I am so glad I refused. Two minutes later, I received another call from my attorney saying that my opponent wants to meet in person to apologize and drop everything! His attorney shared with mine that his client did not want to go to trial and he was a nervous wreck all weekend. Apparently, his client had emailed him frequently throughout the weekend. Whereas my attorney and I barely spoke this whole time. I did not understand why he wanted to meet me in person to apologize, but we all met at my attorney's office. When I met the other attorney he said to me, "It's good to finally meet you in person." I had a chuckle over that comment. We ended up dropping the case about an hour before our jury trial.

Weeks later, I received paperwork in the mail from my attorney. They had sent the paperwork to my old address therefore; I did not receive it until well after the trial date. I found out my attorney was suing him for a lot more than I knew about. As I prayed and worshipped the night before our court date, I felt complete peace. I trusted and believed that God had it all covered and would take care of everything. I was so confident in God and Craig that I read Scripture about not gloating at the fall of our enemies.

I asked God to help me remain humble no matter the outcome and give me a heart that will not gloat at my enemies' fall. He did just that. I don't share a lot of what goes on in my personal life, but I hope that my testimonies give you hope and encourage you to seek the Lord. I hope they encourage you to move beyond the bedtime prayer and dive deeper into God's Word. And better yet, incorporate fasting and prayer. I would like to point out that this person that was taking me to court I had known for over 20 years. We had many friends in the same circle. I did not share this difficult time with our mutual friends because I did not want our friends to feel like they had to choose sides. There were a select few that knew what was going on but for the most part, to this day, many have no idea this happened. I share this bit of information because I think it's important to understand that we, as believers, do not need to react the way the world would expect us to. There is no reason to bad mouth others and definitely no reason to blast it all over social media.

Shadrach, Meshach & Abednego

God had me reading the book of Daniel for many months. If you have not read the book, I strongly recommend that you do. By faith, these three men quenched the violence of the fiery furnace. They did not put out the fire, and they did not destroy the furnace. They just quenched the fire. It's a wondrous thing when a believer can enter into a fire, but the fire cannot enter into him. That is faith.

Our faith is revealed by the light in the fire, not by the songs we sing or even by our prayers. Contrary to what most think, a crisis is not what makes a man strong; a crisis shows what a man is made of. God says when we walk through the fires, we will not be burned. At times it may not feel like you will not be burned by the fire but trust me, don't give up. The Bible is loaded with stories where people fasted and prayed for God's protection and you can do that too. The next time you find yourself in a disconcerting situation, remember that you can put your trust in Jesus to protect and guide you.

Chapter Eleven

Fasting for Deliverance, Breakthrough & Destroying Strongholds

All of us have strongholds in our lives, whether we admit it or not. Many people today are seeking a breakthrough in some area of their life or deliverance from a stronghold. 2 Corinthians 10:4 says, *"For the weapons of our warfare are not carnal but mighty in God for pulling down strongholds."* Notice that Paul used the word weapons in the plural sense, referring to many spiritual weapons. Secondly, notice Paul says weapons of our warfare are not carnal. Carnal pertains to the flesh or being in the natural state. This means the weapons of our warfare are not of man's device or by our human power. What comes to your mind when you hear of spiritual strongholds?

In the next verse, Paul goes on to explain to us what he calls strongholds. 2 Corinthians 10:5 says, *"casting down arguments and every high thing that exalts itself against the knowledge of God, bringing every thought into captivity to the obedience of Christ."* One way Satan comes against us is to attack our minds. One of the main weapons that Paul was referring to is the Word of God. The Word of God is backed by God's Spirit. It is the Word of the Spirit, strong enough to pull down and crush the strongholds of Satan.

If you are struggling in an area, one of your greatest weapons to pull down the strongholds in your life is by the Word of God. You must spend time in the Bible to know what His Word says. If you have been praying for a breakthrough or to be delivered from a stronghold in your life, ask yourself, how much time have I spent reading God's Word? If the answer is not at all or very little, then how can you expect to pull down these strongholds? God's Word says it's not done in the natural. You absolutely need His supernatural power and the power of His Word. One of the benefits of fasting is that this is a perfect time to remove yourself from other distractions and spend time reading the living Word of God.

There are spiritual forces of darkness that strike against all of us. Do not be fooled into believing that you don't matter to them. If you matter to God, you matter to them. Fasting and prayer is sometimes the only thing that will break the yoke of the grip or the bondage in a person's life. As Christians, we are promised power and strength when we call upon the Lord to deliver us from the snares of the enemy. Satan schemes to bind us in many forms. It may be in the form of addictions, fear, worry, our finances, our emotions, our thoughts, our relationships, or maybe a repetitive cycle that you cannot seem to break free from.

Maybe you have been seeking God and praying for deliverance from your endless case of worrying. Some will say that is just the way they are. They are worrywarts. Although the Bible may not explicitly state that worry is a sin, we can conclude from Scripture that it is. If we trust in our worry more than we trust God, we are doing so because of our lack of faith in God. In Matthew Chapter 6, God tells us do not worry. I don't believe it's merely a suggestion.

In 1 Peter, God tells us to submit to God and resist the devil, and he will flee. 1 Peter 5:5-6 says, *"Likewise, you younger people, submit yourselves to your elders. Yes, all of you be submissive to one another, and be clothed with humility, for "God resists the proud, But gives grace to the humble." Therefore, humble yourselves under the mighty hand of God, that He may exalt you in due time, casting all your care upon Him, for He cares for you."*

One of the ways we humble ourselves is through fasting and prayer. Whatever area in your life you need deliverance from, you have to learn to fight in the spiritual first. Satan is real. His minions are real, and the principalities are all real. One of Satan's greatest lies is that he is not real. Satan is not the guy with red horns on his head and a pitched fork like we all pictured him to be when we were children. No, the Bible tells us that he appears as an angel of light.

Spiritual warfare is real even if you can't see it with your physical eyes. To think otherwise is only ignorance. And unlike what the world teaches us that ignorance is bliss, God's Word says otherwise. Ignorance is not going to protect you or save you. There are demonic principalities that carry sickness, disease, accidents, and tragedies. Every accident, sickness, or tragedy that happens, happens in the spirit first. Whatever occurs in the natural occurs in the spiritual first. And before you can tell that mountain where to go in the natural realm, you first have to kill it in the spiritual.

You cannot kill it in the spiritual realm on your own. This is done by God through His Word. People want to skip over this step. They call on their pastors or friends to pray for them, but they skip the most important step. And then people wonder why their prayers are not answered. Some people believe that their pastor's prayer holds more authority than their own. This can be true in some instances, but if you are harnessing unbelief, the prayer from your pastor will not have any more authority than yours would.

As I matured in my walk with Jesus, I learned that fasting is not just about abstaining from food. There was more to it. For example, it was through fasting that I began to spend more time reading the Bible. The more I read, the more notes I took. The more notes I took, the more I began to memorize verses from the Bible. This has been fundamental with helping me to recognize a thought, feeling, or emotion that comes from the enemy. Now I can quickly cast those down and replace them with what God's Word says.

If you have not seen deliverance, I want you to think about something. How can you pull down the strongholds of the enemy if you don't have the strength to turn off your TV or break from social media? How many times a day do we see people sharing their rants on social media or their financial struggles? How many Go Fund Me Pages do we see in a day? I'm not saying that sharing your struggles on social media is all wrong, but why not seek God first? I am only trying to point out that if you spent half as much time in prayer and fasting as you do on your phones, then maybe you would start to see some breakthroughs in your life.

There are many testimonies in Scripture and personal testimonies of people who have fasted and prayed, resulting in great spiritual breakthroughs. What wasn't a reality suddenly was. That unwanted situation or relationship that was there suddenly wasn't. Every person I know needs a breakthrough in some area of their life. I am no exception. I need breakthroughs all the time -- it may be a breakthrough in understanding a situation, a breakthrough answer to a problem, a breakthrough idea, a breakthrough insight, a breakthrough in financial or material provision, a breakthrough in health. I receive breakthrough when I spend time in prayer and fasting. I will share a few of my testimonies below. If you have any need in your life, you need a breakthrough from God to meet that need! Fasting and prayer break the yoke of bondage and brings about a release of God's presence, power, and provision.

Personal Breakthrough Moments

One of the areas I wanted to see a breakthrough in my life was drinking alcohol. It was not that I had partied every weekend or drank every night. The effects of drinking were never consistent with me. One day I could have a glass of wine and felt fine. The next time, I had a glass of wine, and I was drunk. But don't mistake me, I had my years of partying. Although they were fun, I knew I was outside of God's will for my life. The main reason I wanted to quit, though, was because of what God's Word says. There is nothing wrong with drinking alcohol, but God's Word does say we should be of a sober mind. I wanted to be able to have a drink with friends but be able to do so without the buzz or getting drunk. I asked the Lord to help me with this and I received a breakthrough almost immediately. Today, I am able to have a drink without the desire to get that buzz or fall prey to drunkenness. I prefer to have a sober mind.

Another area in my life that I have needed a breakthrough was learning how to let go and let God. When I brought this before the Lord and spent time fasting and praying, the Lord showed me how our lack of understanding can keep us in bondage. The Lord gave me a vision of holding onto a set of reins so tightly that the palms of my hands turned white. This vision reminded me of a time that I was driving through a tornado, and I had gripped the steering wheels so hard that the palms of my hands got sweaty and turned white. During this quiet time with the Lord, He also revealed to me that one of the causes of clenching my jaws was because I was holding onto situations in my life that I should have been releasing to Him.

I have several personal testimonies of when I fully surrendered it all to God, and He answered way beyond what I could have ever imagined. I share a few of them at the end of this book. There have been so many times I had prayed for a mountain in my life to be moved. And when it was not happening fast enough after having spent time in prayer, I felt the need to step in and force the results. I cannot stress enough how much anxiety that has caused in my life. It is true God can turn things around for us, but in my case, it was after I had already experienced the anxiety and stress caused by not trusting God. The reality is, I was suggesting God was not moving fast enough on my behalf, and I could not sit back and wait. In other words, I was taking back control of what

I had surrendered to Him. We often speak the words, let go and let God, but are we letting go? I asked the Lord to show me what it means to surrender it all to Him.

What is complete surrender? Complete surrender requires a willingness to set aside our own appetites and learn to put our trust in the Lord. We can limit what God can do in our lives by our negative attitudes, unbelief, fear, worry, complaining and trying to control everything. When you realize there is no problem in your life right now that you can fix on your own, apart from Jesus, it is easier to surrender it all to the One who can.

Let go of…SELF

When I realized I had no idea what this looked like, I prayed the following prayer, "Alright Lord, You are going to have to show me what this looks like because I have NO idea." The further I dug deeper into what it means to surrender control and let God in, I realized that I was having a hard time trusting that God would act on my behalf. It was hard for me to trust someone that I could not physically see, especially, if I could not see them in action working on my behalf. Whether it was to provide me with opportunities, strategies or answers, I trusted more in my action to produce results than I did in God. Psalm 46:10 says, *"Cease striving and know that I am God; I will be exalted among the nations, I will be exalted in the earth."* (NASB) Striving means to struggle or fight forcefully. To cease striving means to stop struggling, pleading, or contending. In other words, God is saying stop all of that struggling and pleading right now and know that I am God. One way we let go of control is to stop striving.

John 15:4 says, *"Abide in Me, and I in you. As the branch cannot bear fruit of itself unless it abides in the vine, neither can you, unless you abide in Me. I am the vine, you are the branches. He who abides in Me and I in him, he bears much fruit; for without Me you can do nothing."* John 15:7 says, *"If you abide in Me, and My words abide in you, you will ask what you desire, and it shall be done for you."*

If we are abiding in Him, we don't need to stress about how things will work out. If we are abiding in Him, we will bear much fruit. When the Lord spoke to me through those verses, I felt an immense amount of weight lift off of my shoulders. It was at that moment, that I realized, I was struggling (striving) because I was trying to do it all on my own. Realizing, I don't have to figure out every last detail, to its perfection, allowed me to let go. I learned that as long as I am abiding in Jesus, I will bear much fruit. And as long as His Words, are abiding in me, then when I ask what I desire for, it will be done for me. I was reading in the book of Proverbs one day, and the following verses spoke volumes to me. If we are truly seeking the Lord, He will give us the right answers, and our plans will succeed. There is a God-confidence that filled my cup when I believed that my plans will succeed, if I am committing my actions to the Lord.

Proverbs 16 (NLT)

Verse 1 *"We can make our own plans, but the Lord gives the right answer."*

Verse 3 *"Commit your actions to the Lord, and your plans will succeed."*

Verse 9 *"We can make our plans, but the Lord determines our steps."*

Verse 20 *"Those who listen to instruction will prosper; those who trust the Lord will be joyful."*

Verse 21 *"The wise are known for their understanding, and pleasant words are persuasive."*

Verse 33 *"We may throw the dice, but the Lord determines how they fall."*

If you want to learn how to experience prosperity in your life, God's way, then pay close attention to what I am about to share. I have needed a breakthrough in my finances. There have been times when I was down to nothing, and no matter how much I worked, it never seemed like it was enough. When I began to seek the Lord about this, the revelation was so profound that it was a life-changer for me. For years, I had questioned God why so many Christians were not experiencing the promises of God. The Bible says you will know them by their fruit. The problem was, I was not seeing the kind of fruit the Bible talks about in most people's lives, including my own. Instead, I was seeing lack in the lives of so many. I am not only talking material possessions but also, health, peace, joy and patience. And especially so, in the lives of so many Christians. I was determined to get an answer from God and was not going to back down until I did.

I was torn between what the world teaches and what God's Word teaches regarding success and prosperity. As a business owner myself and a drive within me to not live a life of mediocrity, I understood the importance of writing out our dreams, and goals. I also understood the significance of visualization. I believe that if you can conceive it, you can achieve it. Most of the goals I have achieved, were goals that I boldly wrote out on my white board where I could visually see them every single day. The confusion set in when Christian friends tried to convince me that we should not pray for such things as success, financial goals or business goals. This is why it's so important that you know the Bible and have a personal relationship with Jesus. Just because someone claims to know the Bible that does not mean that everything, they say is gospel. This includes pastors, teachers, and authors, including myself. You must learn to search the Bible for yourself and ask God for understanding, knowledge and wisdom.

Ephesians 1:3 says, *"Blessed be the God and Father of our Lord Jesus Christ, who has blessed us with every spiritual blessing in the heavenly places in Christ."* Notice it says, "has" blessed us. This means that God has already blessed us. Past tense. A done deal. But if we are already blessed then why are many Christian's begging and pleading with God to bless them? Most Christians live their entire lives seeking God trying to get Him to bless, heal, deliver, and prosper them. The problem is not with God. If you are not seeing God's promises for you manifesting in your life, it is because you have not yet learned how to receive His blessings. How do you receive God's blessings in your life? Well, you have to know what His Word says first and foremost. If you don't know what God has already promised you through His written Word, then you have no way to believe for His promises or proclaim them over your life. Secondly, you have to learn to believe that God says what He means and means what He says. It's simple really, you have to believe His Word.

Our small mindedness can hold us back from receiving His blessings. I'm sure you have heard prayers like this, God we pray that you be with us today. Yet, the Bible says, that God is always with us, He will never leave us nor forsake us. So why are people praying that way then? Because, they lack knowledge and understanding. Now maybe you pray that way because you are not feeling His presence but that is not on God, that is on you. If you are having a hard time hearing from God or feeling that He is distance, then maybe it's because you need to spend more time in His Word, in prayer or taking a season to fast. How many times have you heard people confess that they are nothing, and they can do nothing? Yet, God's Word tells us that we have the mind of Christ, and we can do all things through Christ who strengthens us. Note that I say through Christ. That does not mean we are gods, like some of the worldly teachings proclaim. Prayers like this fracture your faith and trust in what God has already promised you. The key is to stop asking and get into agreement with God to receive what He has already provided for you.

Any lack in our lives could also be something as simple as our own stinkin' thinkin.' I once read an article that said our negative thoughts are a multiple of four to seven times more powerful than its equivalent. And when we speak things out loud, they are ten times more powerful. For example, when you are thinking about things that you don't want to happen, you are increasing the probability of the exact things you don't want to happen by 40-70 times. Whether this is true or not, I don't know. But I know the Bible says that our thoughts and words are powerful, and we are either speaking life or death into our lives and our circumstances.

God revealed to me that my own stinkin' thinkin' was holding me back from receiving the very best He has for me. One of the stumbling blocks in my life was that I continued to look in the rearview mirror. One day during my prayer time, I saw the words, "Don't Look Back!" I was reminded of the scripture in Genesis 19, where Lot's wife looked back and she became a pillar of salt. And how the Israelites began to complain in the wilderness and suggested they would be better off in Egypt. Even though they would be enslaved again, it was something that was familiar and predictable to them. All but two men that came out of Egypt died in the wilderness and never made it to the Promise Land, because they doubted the Lord.

My past failures, fears, struggles and even longing my past successes were keeping me from receiving God's best for me. The Lord showed me that comments such as, "It's just the way it's always been," has been a roadblock from breaking free from certain repetitive patterns in my life. That simple, yet powerful statement was a stumbling block in my life.

From this revelation I learned a few salt principles:

- Looking back, holds you back.
- Looking back can cause you to stumble.
- Longing your past, delays what lays ahead.

God will provide you with answers when you are earnestly seeking Him. Back in 2017, God put it on my heart to move towards more of a whole foods diet. I was not a hundred percent certain it was from God so I put it on the back burner. A few years later, I found out why He put that on my heart. Had I obeyed Him, I may not have experienced the debilitating peri-menopause that went on for almost a year. This along with PMDD and ADD is not a good mixture. Almost overnight, I changed from a high-energy person to someone who could barely get out of bed. I experienced debilitating fatigue, brain fog, lack of motivation, hives, memory issues, night sweats that soaked my sheets and much more. The doctors told me I was going through peri-menopause and basically told me there was nothing they could do.

When I went back to the doctor later explaining to them that I could not work, they tried to diagnose me with depression. The minute I left their office, I felt the Lord say to me with a stern voice, don't believe that lie! I chose to believe what God spoke to me and quickly rebuked the lie that I was suffering from depression. I had this feeling the Lord was showing me that menopause was not part of His plan. And I had this impression that before the Fall, man did not eat animals. A friend of mine had been given nearly the same message. When we shared our stories with each other, we realized that it was confirmation for both of us that what we both were hearing was from God. After months of my own research and seeking God for answers, I learned that our diet is to blame for many of our health-related issues. I realized that God put this on my heart back in 2017 because He knew what I was about to go through. Changing my diet changed everything for me. Looking back now, I only wished I had obeyed His recommendations a lot sooner. God knew what would help me. I am not suggesting that what works for one, works for everyone. If you are having health-related issues, bring it before the Lord and your doctor.

As far as the promises that God has already promised you according to His written Word, start declaring His promises over your life now. Don't sit back, passively begging God to bless you. You take a stand and defend the victory that God has already promised you. If there is an area where you are lacking then ask God to reveal to you what the roadblock is. If it's your finances or income, it would behoove you to understand God's principles on finances. If you are struggling with your health or healing, then study what God says about healing. By declaring God's promises over your life, you are calling things into existence that God has already provided to you, according to His Word. He wants you to succeed. God blesses us so we can be a blessing to others. He has blessed each of us with different gifts and talents. We all have something to offer to society and to others. But if you are sitting home wallowing in your sorrows because of the lack in your life rather than opening your Bible and spending time in prayer, then you may never see your breakthrough. God will not bless laziness or excuses. You can prosper by using God's principles in your finances, health, relationships and your work. If God has put something on your heart that you believe is from Him, then trust that He will provide a way. Even if you cannot see how, it would even be possible. Keep it in your prayers and if it's from Him, it will come to pass. From my own experiences, when God puts a dream on my heart, rarely is it something I can do on my own without Him. Every single time, it has been something that takes me so far out of my comfort zone, that I don't dare trying to do it on my own. Don't allow yourself to get discouraged if it takes time. Some times when God shares something with us that He wants to do in our lives, it could be years before we see it manifest in the physical realm.

Trust God's Timing

Psalms 106:13 says, *"They soon forgot His works; they did not wait for His counsel."* The Israelites were complaining in the wilderness. They forgot all God had done for them already and quickly began to cry and complain because they thought they were lacking. They did not see what God was seeing. They were not waiting for God's plan to unfold. Instead, they gave into their own cravings. Anytime you try to take matters into your own hands, it can delay God's promises for you.

Another example of not waiting on God's timing was Abraham and Sarah. God told Abraham that He would have a son of his own. But rather than waiting on God, Sarah told Abraham to sleep with her slave, Hagar, and if she had a child, it would be hers. They took matters into their own hands. They got so obsessed with making the dream happen that Abraham had a baby with Sarah's slave, Hagar. God was not going to accept their doing as the son that God had promised them. Now they were going to be waiting even longer before they had the son that God promised them. It would not be until Abraham's son by Hagar, turned thirteen, that Sarah would finally get pregnant. When God gives us a dream or a promise, it is so easy for that dream to consume our lives.

Like the Israelites in the wilderness or Abraham and Sarah, we get impatient waiting on God's timing. We do not see the big picture. We are not seeing what God is seeing. And then we take matters into our hands and try to force the dream or promise to happen much sooner than God's timing. There are decisions we make that can cause the dream to be delayed. Idolatry is something that takes God's place. Our dreams or desires can become an idol. Be careful to not become more obsessed with the promise than you are with God. When God wants to do something great with you, He obsesses over your character. Character is the foundation upon which God places on all promises. God will test your character, and there is no way around it. When you become so obsessed with your dreams, goals, or the trials you are going through, it takes the focus away from God.

The Israelites had witnessed God's miracles and provisions, but it was not enough. It became not enough when they took their eyes off Him and His provisions that they had at the moment. Because they complained about not having meat to eat, God did grant them the desires of their heart, but it made them sick. Are you willing to wait to receive God's best for you or choose to receive the desires of your heart right now like the Israelites did? God can provide the desires of your heart right now, outside of His timing, but are you willing to accept the "less than" His best for you? The Israelites complaining and not giving thanks to God, despite their circumstances, angered the Lord. When we give thanks to God despite our circumstances, this truly honors Him.

When the Lord puts something on your heart that He wants to do in your life, trusting in His timing is important. It is equally important to know when it's time for you to take action. God does not tell us to sit around and wait for things to happen. He will not do it for you. This is why you need to make the time to spend in prayer and fasting. How could you possibly hear when the Lord speaks to you if you don't make time to be alone with Him? He will confirm to you when it's time to make your move.

Like Moses parting the Red Sea, his response was to wait on the Lord, but when the Lord instructed him to make his move, Moses had to do it. God wasn't going to strike the ground with the rod for him. And only then did God part the Red Sea. We have all experienced our own Red Sea circumstances. It only stands to reason that in a Red Sea circumstance to be fearful. But God's Word says to be fearless. As a believer, that is indwelt by the very Spirit of God, you have to make a decision to not allow yourself to succumb to fear that can easily overtake you. Another example, is when God asked Job to pray for his friends. Job had to pray for his friends first and then God restored everything

Job had lost and blessed him with even more. Obeying the Lord, waiting on the Lord, and taking action when He gives you instructions are important.

Trusting God After Tragedy

I was watching a story on TV about this couple, a pastor and his wife who lost their child. My heart ached for the pain they suffered. Their feelings of loss, the hurt they described, and wondering how God could allow something like this. The pastor said he had counseled many people and read scriptures on loss, but he never really understood that pain until he lost his own son. He had compassion on others, of course, maybe even knew the right words to say, but it was not until he experienced that kind of loss that he could relate to that kind of pain.

He was thrust into that tension between trusting God and not knowing what's going on. He explained that tragedy teaches us how small we are. We think we get to run this world, and we walk around with the illusion of control, believing that if I live right, get right, and do right, God will bless me. That God will insulate us or put a bubble around us. So, if we don't have control over our lives or those we love, how do we put our trust in the One who does? As I listened intently to their story, I understood what he was saying: if we live right, then bad things will not happen to us.

I believed this for many years. When tough times hit me, I questioned what I did wrong. I assumed God was mad at me. The enemy put thoughts in my head that God was punishing me. We live in a fallen world, and bad things do happen. To all of us, no matter how well we live our lives. The enemy is also a big fat liar. God is not punishing us. Our sins are forgiven if we have confessed our sins to the Lord and repented. God says He remembers them no more. It is Satan who reminds us of our sins. There is a difference between the Holy Spirit convicting us of our sins to turn from our sin and the enemy condemning us. As the story went on, the pastor's wife admitted she used to judge people for having anxiety attacks and depression.

I could relate to this also because I did the same thing. I used to believe that depression and anxiety were all in the mind and could be controlled. I thought people just used depression as an excuse not to perform. It was not until I fell into some hard times myself and realized depression is no joke and it's very real. Depression is not something that is easily overcome on our own. It does not go away by being positive. Although, it was short-lived for me, it was still painful. I took some time off to really seek God for help. I spent a lot of time in prayer, fasting and reading my Bible. God did pull me out of it. He carried me through it and gave me strength when I had none.

Book of Job

Have you ever had a season in your life where you felt like Job? I read Job several times in the past. I knew that the ending of Job was important. In the book of Job, thirty-seven of the chapters are of Job complaining to God. Job kept saying he did not deserve this. Job's theology was if you do right, you get right. Sound familiar? I certainly used to believe this. I believed that the enemy could not touch me, that harm could not come my way, that tragedy or loss would not touch me.

In the story mentioned above about the pastor and his wife losing their child, the pastor was asked what he did to trust God after such a loss. He responded that he had to get reacquainted with God. He said the blinders were lifted from his eyes, and he is seeing God's Word differently now. Trials and tragedy have a way of causing us to seek the Lord more intently.

One of the hardest lessons I have learned was accepting that being a Christian does not make us immune to bad things happening. I honestly believed that if I lived right, did right, that I would somehow escape the major trials or tragedies in life. This is not true. We live in a fallen world and bad things happen. How do we keep our trust in God during trials and tragedies?

For me, it was no longer about blaming God. Or accusing Him of not loving me, or forsaking me, or asking Him how He could allow this? The shift for me was understanding God's character and how He relates to us. Towards the end of the book of Job, God responded to Job about how He created everything. He went into detail about all that He created and how they obey His voice. About how things function and how could we understand it all? We may not understand all things, but God does. If we trust Him, have courageous faith, then He will carry us through such tragedies.

Job 42:5 says, *"I have only heard about you before, but now I have seen you with my own eyes. I take back everything I said, and I sit in dust and ashes to show my repentance."* Before this, Job had nothing but hearsay knowledge of God that was passed down from his forefathers. Job had heard of God but had not yet discovered God. Many today have heard of God but don't know Him or they reject what they hear. There is a point of revelation that must come where your belief changes from theory to reality.

Fasting and prayer is a powerful Christian discipline that will help you obtain deliverance and breakthrough in your life. Many believers struggle with things in their life that they are not able to overcome on their own. It may be poverty, sickness, sexual impurity, fear, control, unbelief, witchcraft, or additions. Whatever, it is, maybe it's time to develop a season of fasting and begin to claim victory over your life. Start believing that God's Word is real. Reading the Bible, believing and declaring God's promises for your life, will change your life.

Chapter Twelve

Fasting is Spiritual Warfare

Fasting combined with prayer and God's Word makes up the most critical weapons of spiritual warfare. What is spiritual warfare? Ephesians 6:12 says, *"For we do not wrestle against flesh and blood, but against principalities, against powers, against the rulers of darkness of this age, against spiritual hosts of wickedness in the heavenly places."*

What is spiritual warfare?

Spiritual warfare is a battle against Satan, the principalities, powers, and rulers of the darkness of this world that takes place in the spiritual dimension or the unseen world. Spiritual warfare is fought with the weapons of divine power to demolish strongholds. We demolish arguments against the knowledge of God and take captive every thought to make it obedient to Christ.

Who is Satan?

Revelation 12:9 describes Satan as the great dragon that was cast out. *"So the great dragon was cast out, that serpent of old, called the Devil and Satan, who deceives the whole world; he was cast to the earth, and his angels were cast out with him."*

Isaiah 14:12 says that Satan is a fallen angel. Satan is invisible, but he is not fictional, and he disguises himself as an angel of light. He is a thief who comes only to kill, steal, and destroy. Spiritual warfare is real, and not believing in spiritual warfare does not protect you from Satan's attacks. The Bible speaks of spiritual warfare in many places. Satan will use every tactic possible to get our focus off God and onto ourselves. His primary weapons are deception and temptation. The Bible tells us that Satan deceives by counterfeiting the true work of the Holy Spirit with lying signs and wonders. He lures people into his schemes with promises of pleasure and power that will satisfy your appetite, which is a lie. And it always comes at the highest price.

So how do we fight against spiritual warfare? Ephesians 6:10 tells us we do this by putting on the full armor of God. When dealing with deception, our two greatest weapons are the belt of truth and the sword of the Spirit, which is the Word of God. You use the belt of truth, the Word of God, to guard against Satan's lies and deception that he sends your way. And you use the sword of the Spirit to tear down strongholds that take residence in your mind. A stronghold is a deception that has taken hold in a person's mind. For example, it could be a lie that you believe about yourself.

Temptation is when we are lured into sin. For example, Satan tempted Jesus in the wilderness, and Jesus resisted the temptation by speaking God's Word. However, when Satan tempted Jesus in the wilderness and Eve in the garden, he used God's Word but twisted God's Word. I want to point that out because even Satan knows God's Word, and just because someone has memorized Scripture does not always mean their motives are pure.

Possible signs or symptoms that you may be under spiritual attack

1. Confusion
2. Depression
3. Distraction
4. Doubt
5. Erratic behavior
6. Isolation
7. Loss of hope
8. Loss of peace
9. Resentment towards God
10. Sudden onslaught of trouble, losses
11. Suicidal
12. Temptations
13. Unusual fatigue
14. Unusual illnesses
15. Weakened faith
16. Withdrawal

As I was writing this chapter, a spiritual attack came against me. This attack was an attempt to steal my joy and a distraction. I had received a call from one of my friends to inform me that they chose to work with another Realtor. This was after they left me believing for the past few months that I would be the one to represent them in their home buying process. To make matters worse, I saw them every day because they were my neighbors and good friends with my son. Their explanation for not hiring me to represent them in the purchase of their new home was that it was a business decision. They felt that because I did not live in the area where they wanted to purchase a home, another Realtor would better represent them.

They were purchasing a home 45 minutes away, which is not that far. I received this call just days before they were scheduled to close on their new home. I was honest with them and told them I was hurt. They reluctantly admitted it might have been a selfish act on their part. I think what hurt the most is how close my son is to them and how much my son has done for them. After I hung up with them, I had mixed emotions. I was hurt and almost in tears. I needed this closing. At this point, it had been a while since my last closing, and my funds were extremely low. This meant no Christmas presents for my son or family this year. I shared the news with my son, and because he is friends with them, he was quite upset. After I received this phone call, I wanted to call one of my close friends with hopes that she could calm me down. However, my phone would not work. It locked up completely.

The number pad would not work; no calls could go in or out. I shut it off a few times, and still nothing. Because this is not something that typically happens to my phone, I figured the Lord must be trying to get my attention. So, I said, ok Lord, I will pray first before I call my friend. Only after I prayed did my phone work. Going into prayer first was critical because the Lord softened my heart. And by the time I did speak to my friend about it, I was not as upset and hurt. Had I been, the conversation would have involved both of us talking bad about these so-called friends of ours.

As I shared with my friend what just happened, I realized at that very moment that this was nothing else but a spiritual attack. And I believe this spiritual attack came at that very moment for two reasons. The first reason was because that day was the day, I committed to focusing on writing this book. The second reason is because of this very chapter, Fasting for Spiritual Warfare. This phone call came just two hours after I started working on this book, and it happened at the very moment I was writing this chapter. That is no coincidence.

I believe that had fasting and prayer not been a big part of my life, I would have handled this situation much differently. From similar past experiences, this would have stolen my joy and would have affected me for days or even weeks. Instead, when I realized this was an attack from the enemy, I thanked Jesus for showing me. I quickly resisted the devil and ordered him to flee. I quickly thanked God for all the blessings in my life. God had softened both mine and my son's hearts towards this couple. My son and I remain friends with them today. I did not let the enemy ruin our friendship.

I prayed, Lord, this is not my battle to fight. It is Yours! I trust You! You do what you want with it. And what the enemy has stolen from me, I want it back, In Jesus Name. That is just one example of a spiritual attack. Spiritual attacks can happen that quick and end that quickly. Some may think that this setback for me was not really a big deal. But, losing out on a $12,000 commission check meant the difference between being able to pay our bills that month or not and being able to buy Christmas gifts for my son. Spiritual warfare is being mindful of the attacks and knowing how to fight back. I believe in this situation the enemy was tempting me to fall prey to his tactics as well as an attempt to steal my joy and ruin a friendship.

There have been times I have just come out of prayer and had a marvelous time with the Lord, only to stub my toe on the way out the door. Something as little as that can easily steal your joy quickly if you allow it. I am going to share a few other situations that happened to me recently. God had been working on me for some time to write this book. The first day I committed to writing this book, only one paragraph came to me. It would be another two months before I sat down to write again. The stirring in my spirit to write grew stronger and stronger each day that it got to the point that I could barely focus on anything else. I finally said, "Ok Lord, I hear You! I will make time today." I got all my chores done first thing in the morning so there would be no distractions. I had just sat down and opened my laptop, and there was a knock on my door. I figured it was just a neighbor dropping something off. It was not one of my neighbors. Instead, it was someone I had met several months prior. I had only met him and his wife one time, therefore, I did not recognize who he was until he told me.

I met them both on a walk before, and they invited me to go to church with them one time. I felt obligated to invite him in because he did not come right out and tell me why he stopped by unannounced. Most people do not just show up unannounced, so I was a bit perplexed. But I grew up in a home where our door was always open to visitors. So, I invited him into my home, wondering if this was a divine appointment from God. But there was a part of me that felt uneasy. Unfortunately, he shared with me that his wife had passed away shortly after I met them both.

The visit lasted about 3 hours, and I was too tired to write by the time he left. I will admit I was bothered by the long visit because it took away from my writing time. After the visit, I was sure this was not a divine appointment from the Lord. Instead, I think it was the enemy trying to distract me from writing in my book that day, at which point he succeeded. One of the clues that this was not from the Lord was the timing of it all. I had only met this guy one time, so essentially, he was a stranger to me. Yet, he showed up at a single woman's home unannounced.

He was also much older than me by at least 30 years. He also admitted that he had driven by my place a few other times because he was lonely. However, he had not stopped by because he could not remember which place was mine. This day, he ran into one of my neighbors outside and asked her if she knew me. He only remembered my first name. My neighbor figured he was a friend, so she directed him to my place. At the end of our visit, he asked me if I would like to go to dinner with him. I had a feeling this guy was interested in more than just being friends, so I thanked him and politely declined.

I want to share another personal testimony of a spiritual attack and how we fought this one with God's Word. My next-door neighbor and I were dealing with another neighbor who was heavily involved in witchcraft, even though she claimed to be a Christian. Not having been exposed to anything like this before, my friend and I were not familiar with witchcraft. But with some of the bizarre things that were happening in our neighborhood and to other neighbors, we got ourselves as familiar as we could. And we prayed a lot! The more we learned about it, the more we prayed over our neighborhood and our neighbors.

One day my friend confronted this neighbor of ours about her involvement in witchcraft, and she did not deny any of it. In fact, this neighbor told my friend that if she told anyone about it, she would be sorry. My friend called me shortly after their conversation to tell me about it. The reason she called to tell me about it is because we had been fasting and praying over the chaos our neighbor was causing. While we were on the phone with each other, there was suddenly a loud banging on my walls. It was so intense that it rattled the pictures on my walls and moved my sofa. My dog and I were sitting on the sofa, and when it moved, my dog got up and started barking. All I could think was she must have known that we were talking about her.

My friend could hear the noise from her home, and she lived directly across from me. This was not something that a human being could do on their own strength. It was a demonic entity and undoubtedly ticked off. At first, I felt fear come over me but then immediately began to pray. We both prayed and began to speak God's Word out loud. I suddenly began to feel dizzy. I ran to my son's room to grab him so we could pray out loud together. I was light-headed for at least an hour. The loud banging noise and my walls shaking went on for about an hour. Everything was happening so fast, and I was also in the middle of cooking spaghetti dinner.

My friend and I hung up so she could go outside to pray over our neighborhood, and my son and I prayed inside our home. At one point, my dog started choking excessively and could barely breathe. I had never seen my dog choke like that before. My son and I immediately prayed over our dog. I pleaded the blood of Jesus over him and commanded whatever that thing was to come out of my dog. After a few moments of this, he finally threw up some green liquid. Right afterward, he went back to being his spunky self.

It was so bizarre. My son and I witnessed the power of the Holy Spirit that night and the mighty power of God's Words. I would be okay if I never had to see that kind of thing again. However, I am grateful my son was with me during this strange incident because now he knows how to come against spiritual attacks. And how to stand in God's power, knowing that we have the power of the Holy Spirit living on this inside of us.

The neighbor that I was on the phone with was outside praying Psalms 91, and my son and I prayed Psalm 91 in our home. The shaking and loud banging noise finally stopped. My dog was fine, and the dizziness I experienced was gone. I have never in my life experienced anything like this, ever! This was my first real experience in dealing with someone that was involved in witchcraft and Santeria. After this experience, my son and I decided it was best to continue to pray over our home, ourselves and our neighborhood frequently. A few times, when I did see her outside, she appeared to be in some kind of trance.

I'm not all that familiar with trances, but I was told when we see her like that it's best not to approach her.

One time she was white as a ghost with dark circles around her eyes. I have never seen anyone look like this before, except for in the movies. Several other neighbors had witnessed her in this state as well. Her look and demeaner was nothing short of disturbing. Naturally, we all kept our distance when she looked like that. I am grateful for God's promises that He will never leave us nor forsake us. The weapons you use to battle spiritual warfare are not physical but are spiritual. You need the Word of God to pull down strongholds and battle spiritual warfare. Fasting combined with prayer can help prepare you to have complete victory over the enemy and his schemes. I knew enough to understand that the battle was not against this woman. It was against the enemy who just happened to have a hold-in this woman's life. Because of this, I kept my distance from her but prayed for her often.

This is the same lady that I spoke of in an earlier chapter. Thankfully, she had moved away not long after all of this happened. I do believe that because we were faithfully praying over her, over our neighbors and our neighborhood that God was protecting all of us. There was so much more that happened because of this lady but that is too much to share in this book. Spiritual warfare is not something to be afraid of. I think we need to be mindful of it but don't obsess over it. In my opinion, people can get carried away with putting too much focus on spiritual warfare. From my own experience, most of the spiritual warfare I battle is within the mind. The enemy loves to attack our minds.

If you are a born-again believer and have the Holy Spirit living on the inside of you, remember the verse in 1 John 4 that says, He that lives in you is greater than he that lives in this world. You have the Holy Spirit living on the inside of you, don't forget that! Jesus has won the battle against the enemy, which means you can have complete victory over spiritual warfare. God is not going to do it for you. You have to learn how to fight spiritual warfare and be confident in God's spoken Word over your life.

Chapter Thirteen

God Responds to Fasting and Prayer

I grew up believing that prayer alone changes everything. Although prayer is powerful and a critical discipline in a Christian's life, prayer alone is sometimes not enough. I can think of many things I had prayed for, sometimes for long periods of time, only to feel disappointed that I was not receiving direction from the Lord. As well as not receiving a breakthrough in some area of my life or deliverance from a situation. I have cried out to God with desperation, and although I would often feel comforted and feel some peace after reading Scripture, there was still something missing.

When God first began to speak to me about fasting, I did not take it as seriously as I do now. As I began to dig deeper into studying the principles of fasting, I realized it's something much bigger than I could have imagined. Like many of you, I keep myself busy. Fasting is one of the disciplines where I slow down enough to hear God's small quiet voice. There are massive benefits to humbling yourself before the Lord. When you do this, you allow God to do for you what you cannot do on your own. God will give you strategy when you are fasting.

Sometimes you don't need more resources but instead, what you need is strategy. Ezra needed strategy; therefore, he proclaimed a fast. Ezra 8:21-23 says, *"Then I proclaimed a fast there at the river of Ahava, that we might humble ourselves before our God, to seek from Him the right way for us and our little ones and all of our possessions. For I was ashamed to request of the king an escort of soldiers and horsemen to help us against the enemy on the road, because we had spoken to the king, saying, "The hand of our God is upon all those for good who seek Him, but His power and His wrath are against all those who forsake Him." So, we fasted and entreated our God for this, and He answered our prayer."* Let's dig deeper into why Ezra called for fast prior to this journey. Ezra was leading a group of the exiled Israelites back to Jerusalem from Babylon. They would be carrying with them millions of dollars' worth of provisions. The king is the one that sanctioned this move back to Israel, and he offered to provide troops and horsemen to help protect against the enemy on the road. Ezra declined the offered help and protection because he wanted the people to know that this move was of God and not of man and that God would protect them.

Had Ezra accepted the king's offer for the soldiers to journey with them and protect them, the people would not have witnessed God delivering them from the hand of the enemy. In verse 31, it states that the hand of God was upon them, and He delivered them from the hand of the enemy and from ambush along the road. God was a vital part of that journey. When we fast, we are strengthening our relationship with God. Answered prayers are a product of a strong relationship with God and the right alignment to His will. By submitting yourself in fasting and prayer, you also submit your own will to His.

Throughout the Bible, it is evident that God responds to fasting. Fasting is a gift from God. Too often people turn to other people or resources for answers rather than seeking God for council first. God responds to fasting and prayer because when you fast, you are taking the focus off of yourself and other resources. As you look to Jesus as your only hope, you are admitting your need for Jesus and expressing your trust in Him.

When you spend time fasting and in prayer, you should also spend time meditating on God's Word. The more time you spend in God's Word, your faith is strengthened. Faith comes by hearing and hearing the Word of God. (Romans 10:17) Prayer that brings results is based on God's Word. Jesus said in John 15:7, *"If you abide in Me, and My words abide in you, you will ask what you desire, and it shall be done for you."* Prayers go unanswered for many reasons, but fasting with prayer can clear up any confusion. The Bible is full of promises that apply to any one of your situations, including wisdom, health, success, wealth, protection, fear, worry, and victory.

Chapter Fourteen

What is Done in Private, God Will Reward Publicly

According to Matthew 6:17-18, it is not necessary for others to know we are fasting. It's really between you and God. There are times when we may need to inform others, especially those we live with, but the point is we don't need to advertise it. Matthew 6:17-18 says, *"But you, when you fast, anoint your head and wash your face, so that you do not appear to men to be fasting, but to your Father who is in the secret place; and your Father who sees in secret will reward you openly."* When you do this in secret, God will reward you openly. I will be honest with you that when I first began to fast, I did so with a bit of a prideful spirit.

I'm sure you know what I am talking about. When people ask you why you are not eating, and you proudly announce that you are fasting. Being spiritually proud of the fact that you are fasting will destroy everything you are trying to accomplish. Jesus made it clear that when you fast and talk too much about it, looking distressed due to depriving yourself so that others will think you are super-spiritual, you will indeed receive your reward, which is the attention of other people. But if you fast to your Father, who is in the secret place, your Father will reward you openly.

You can't have it both ways. You don't want to get caught up in being too legalistic about it, either. Jesus did not say that no one should ever find out about your fasting. He was more concerned with your heart. Rather than focusing on the fast for attention or recognition, conduct your fast unto the Lord. I once read never to be envious of a blessed person because you have no idea what they have done in secret. You have no idea what sacrifices they went through to get there. This is similar to the kind of people that express their jealousy by criticizing highly successful entrepreneurs. People criticize others for spending thousands of dollars on a vehicle or having two homes or a private jet. Yet those same people criticizing are the same people who are not willing to put in the many extra hours or additional education. They are not willing to wake up before everyone else does. The majority of successful entrepreneurs in the world do not spend hours in the evening watching television. To be that successful, it takes sacrifice and serious discipline.

Yet, those who criticize are not willing to cancel cable so they can focus on other things that would produce a better lifestyle. How about those who criticize the people that work out all the time and eat healthy? Yet, they are not willing to wake up at 5 am to work out every day or remain disciplined with healthy eating habits. Instead, they criticize those who do and make judgements. Ironically, I have found that those criticizing are usually the very people who are overweight. I have heard from many people that think everything naturally falls into place for me, and they think I have had it so easy. People have said to me, you make good money, so it's easy for you. The truth? The truth is none of it came easy for me. I had to work a lot extra hours some weeks to make that happen. Most of what I do is behind the scenes. I don't have time to share all of my struggles or successes on social media because I am too busy living a productive life. Also, I do not feel the victim mentality serves anyone well.

Another time when it's better to do things in private is when you give. Matthew 6:1-4 says, *"Take heed that you do not do your charitable deeds before men, to be seen by them. Otherwise, you have no reward from your Father in heaven. Therefore, when you do a charitable deed, do not sound a trumpet before you as the hypocrites do in the synagogues and in the streets, that they may have glory from men. Assuredly, I say to you, they have their reward. But when you do a charitable deed, do not let your left hand know what your right hand is doing, that your charitable deed may be in secret; and your Father who sees in secret will Himself reward you openly."*

I often see people blasting all over social media how they paid for someone's groceries because someone's card was declined at check out. Or they bought a homeless person a meal or gave someone in need some cash. When we give, we should give not to be seen by others. Some people claim they make these announcements because they hope that it will encourage others to do the same. I suppose I can see how it may encourage others, but if they are completely honest with themselves, they are doing it to receive applause from other people. There is nothing humbling about that behavior.

We all want other people to know that we have a giving heart and are good people. But God's Word says that when people act this way, they will surely receive the rewards they are looking for, which are compliments and applause from others. But when we do things in secret, God says He will reward us publicly. Wouldn't you rather receive a reward from your Heavenly Father than from men?

When you fast, try to keep it between you and the Lord. This is your time together with your Heavenly Father. If you find it hard to say no to food at events, then kindly excuse yourself or decline the offer. If someone invites you out to lunch during your fast, maybe suggest meeting for coffee or tea instead. There will be situations where you will have to just let someone know that you are on a fast right now. One thing I have found most beneficial when I am about to go on a fast is preparation. If you know you are going to do a fast in a few days, then try to do as much preparation as you can ahead of time. For example, plan to block out some time, and change your voice mail if you have to. Try to find someone to watch your children if it's just a few hours fast. Make sure you have your Bible, notebook, a few pens, highlighters, a bottle of water, and whatever else you might need.

Whatever you are seeking the Lord for during your fast, pray for His direction. It's a good idea to keep a journal and write down what you believe you are hearing from the Lord. And if He directs you to a Scripture, read it, meditate on it, and write down your thoughts. Even if it doesn't mean much to you right now, it could be something later. I do believe God wants us to share our testimonies with others. Testimonies are powerful. Therefore, I feel it's important to keep a journal of what you have learned or heard from the Lord during your time of prayer and fasting. There may be something you can share with others that will give others hope and encouragement. I would like to end this chapter with this. The next time you begin to feel envious because of someone's blessed life, remember that you don't know what they have done in secret to get there. The next time you are fasting or blessing someone in need, remember that God rewards publicly, what you do in private. We do not fast or give to those in need for selfish reasons. It should always be done with a humble heart and to glorify God, not yourself.

Chapter Fifteen

Be Intentional About Your Fast

It is important to know why you are fasting. Sometimes you might choose to fast because you desire a deeper intimacy with God or because you are seeking Him over a specific issue. Other times, God might call you to a fast as an act of faith and obedience. Identifying why you are doing it is significant because it helps you focus, especially when the fast becomes difficult. During the discomfort, you can fix your eyes on why it is going to be worth it. A fast is not because you forget to eat a meal. To enter a fast after you've realized you have skipped a meal is not being intentional. How serious are you about getting results?

Whether we are talking about your career, education, goals, weight loss, or training for a marathon, you must be intentional to see solid results. Fasting is no different. When you are ready to start a fast, don't enter your fast casually or passively. Plan to succeed. Tell God that you are coming after Him with all of your heart. You cannot go about fasting by saying to yourself, I will see how I feel and how long I can make it. Instead, you take a firm stand, or you will not fast successfully. You make up your mind and proclaim to yourself and the Lord that you are going to do a breakfast fast tomorrow or going on a three-day or seven-day fast.

Whatever fast you choose, or the Holy Spirit puts on your heart, do it with intention. Imagine how different our lives would be if we spent as much time focusing on God as we do about many of the nonproductive activities that don't bear good fruit in our lives. Do you think your life would change if you learned to live a fasted life? When I first began to fast, much of my fasts were done passively. I started out with the idea that I was going to do a three-day water-only fast. As time got closer to my fasting day, I found myself changing it to a liquid-only fast so I could at least have chicken broth. And would you know it, during my fast, I thought it to be no big deal that I ate a cracker here and there. It is not my belief that God suddenly shut the door on me because I ate a cracker. Instead, I believe He appreciated the effort and the fact that I was learning about this Christian discipline. If at first you find that fasting is too difficult, there are some things that helped me get past that hurdle. Plan your fast. I like to plan my fast a day or a few days ahead of time. This helps me to prepare for the fast mentally and to get things in order.

Depending on your situation, you can start slow. Rather than committing to a 21-day liquid-only fast, start with a 1–3-day liquid-only fast. Pray before you fast. When I go on a longer fast, I start praying about the fast many days beforehand. Ask the Lord to guide you, to give you strength, and it's a good idea to ask Him if there is anything in your heart that you need to settle before you begin your fast. He may reveal something to you about pride, wrong motives, or unforgiveness that needs to be dealt with.

There is something to be said about entering a fast with purpose and intent. We will all have different experiences. Which is why, I feel its important that we don't compare our experiences or results with other people's results. I can be hard-headed and impatient at times. When I first started to incorporate fasting into my Christian walk, I did not see results. I felt discouraged and even envious of how others seemed to get results much faster than me. It was difficult for me to be still and quiet for a period of time. It caused a great deal of anxiety for me. I got impatient and threw my hands up in the air and said, I'm sorry Lord, but I have had enough of this sitting still. If you want me to hear You, then You must learn to speak to me a lot quicker.

As if I had the right to tell God He doesn't communicate fast enough. As time went on, I learned to be patient and quiet my mind. Only then did I begin to hear God speak to me. My point to sharing this, is that for some of us, it may take longer to start seeing the rewards from spending time in fasting and prayer. I promise you though, if you don't give up, you will start to see a shift take place in your heart, mind and in your life.

Chapter Sixteen

Living a Fasted Life

So far, we have talked about what biblical fasting is and is not, the different types of fasting, the duration of fasting, and the benefits of fasting. Now we are going to talk about what God says about fasting and how He feels about the Christian discipline of fasting. Last year, when I thought, I was finished writing this book God had other plans.

As I was ready to put the final touches on my manuscript, God took me to Isaiah 58 and spoke to me through this chapter in a way that was so profound. Let's take a look at what God is telling His people in Isaiah 58. Typically, I read from the NKJV, but we will be reading this Scripture from the New Living Translation version.

Isaiah 58 New Living Translation (NLT)

True and False Worship

"Shout with the voice of a trumpet blast. Shout aloud! Don't be timid. Tell
my people Israel of their sins! 2 Yet they act so pious! They come to the Temple
every day and seem delighted to learn all about me. They act like a righteous
nation that would never abandon the laws of its God. They ask me to take action
on their behalf, pretending they want to be near me. 3 'We have fasted before
you!' they say. 'Why aren't you impressed? We have been very hard on
ourselves, and you don't even notice it!' "I will tell you why!" I respond. "It's
because you are fasting to please yourselves. Even while you fast, you keep
oppressing your workers. 4 What good is fasting when you keep on fighting and
quarreling? This kind of fasting will never get you anywhere with me. 5You
humble yourselves by going through the motions of penance, bowing your
heads like reeds bending in the wind. You dress in burlap and cover yourselves
with ashes. Is this what you call fasting? Do you really think this will please
the Lord? 6 "No, this is the kind of fasting I want:

Free those who are wrongly imprisoned; lighten the burden of those who work for you. Let the oppressed go free and remove the chains that bind people. [7] Share your food with the hungry and give shelter to the homeless. Give clothes to those who need them, and do not hide from relatives who need your help. [8] "Then your salvation will come like the dawn, and your wounds will quickly heal. Your godliness will lead you forward, and the glory of the Lord will protect you from behind. [9] Then when you call, the Lord will answer. 'Yes, I am here,' he will quickly reply. "Remove the heavy yoke of oppression. Stop pointing your finger and spreading vicious rumors!

[10] Feed the hungry and help those in trouble. Then your light will shine out from the darkness, and the darkness around you will be as bright as noon. [11] The Lord will guide you continually, giving you water when you are dry and restoring your strength. You will be like a well-watered garden, like an ever-flowing spring. [12]Some of you will rebuild the deserted ruins of your cities. Then you will be known as a rebuilder of walls and a restorer of homes. [13] "Keep the Sabbath day holy. Don't pursue your own interests on that day but enjoy the Sabbath and speak of it with delight as the Lord's holy day. Honor the Sabbath in everything you do on that day, and don't follow your own desires or talk idly. [14] Then the Lord will be your delight. I will give you great honor and satisfy you with the inheritance I promised to your ancestor Jacob. I, the Lord, have spoken!"

"[1]Shout with the voice of a trumpet blast. Shout aloud! Don't be timid. Tell my people Israel of their sins!

In verse 1, the Lord speaks loudly about the sins of His people. He is saying, shout loudly and don't be timid to tell My people about their sins! The Lord is telling the prophet Isaiah to shout, to "call with the throat," which means to call with all his voice. He is not telling Isaiah to speak to them gently. The purpose of getting the people's attention is to make them aware of their rebellion.

They did not understand the scope of their sins, therefore, did not have a clue as to the remedy of their sins. If you remain unaware of your sins, how will you know what the remedy is to your situation? There is a correlation between our unrepented sins and God not responding to our fasting and prayers. The good news is that when you earnestly seek the Lord, He will reveal what the barrier is.

[2] Yet they act so pious! They come to the Temple every day and seem delighted to learn all about me. They act like a righteous nation that would never abandon the laws of its God. They ask me to take action on their behalf, pretending they want to be near me.

In verse 2, God is calling His people out on their sins and the appearance they are portraying. It was void of true worship and fasting. On the surface, they look like they are doing everything right. They appear to be delighted to learn all about God. They appear as though they have never abandoned the laws of God. Yet, they ask God to take action on their behalf, pretending like they want to be near God. In other versions, the words "as" or "as if" are used, indicating that the Lord is making it clear that the people have not been faithful and true to God's laws.

They are asking God to act on their behalf. The irony is that these unrighteous people are asking God for righteous judgments, yet they fail to understand that if God were to render righteous judgments, they would be vindicated as well. How many Christians today pretend to want to be near to God? Have you caught yourself saying that you want to be near to God but do not take action to do so? There comes a point where you have to move beyond other people spoon feeding you the Word. Where you are not dependent on other people to tell you what the Word of God says. If you really want to know your Heavenly Father and be close to Him, you must spend time reading the Bible, meditating on His Word, and humbling yourself in fasting and prayer.

[3] 'We have fasted before you!' they say. 'Why aren't you impressed? We have been very hard on ourselves, and you don't even notice it!'

In verse 3, they were asking God why their prayers were going unanswered and why hasn't God taken notice of their fasting. They sound like quite the crybabies, don't they? God answers that in the next verse. But let's focus on their complaint first. They had fasted from food to demonstrate their repentance and to honor God. They were whining that they have been hard on themselves. They believed that if they devoted to fast, then God was obligated to reward and bless them. Fasting does not obligate God to anything. Fasting is not works-based but rather it's an act of selflessness. Fasting is hungering for God.

[3] "I will tell you why!" I respond. "It's because you are fasting to please yourselves. But, even while you fast, you keep oppressing your workers.

[4] What good is fasting when you keep on fighting and quarreling? This kind of fasting will never get you anywhere with me. [5] You humble yourselves by going through the motions of penance, bowing your heads like reeds bending in the wind. You dress in burlap and cover yourselves with ashes. Is this what you call fasting? Do you really think this will please the Lord?

In verses 3-5, God tells them exactly why He was not impressed, and why their prayers went unanswered. His firm response, I will tell you why, would certainly get my attention. It was because the fasting they were doing was to please themselves. And while they were portraying that they had been obedient to God's laws, they continued to mistreat their workers. They continued to fight and quarrel with each other. God says that kind of fasting will never get them or us anywhere with Him. They dressed the part in order to appear to men to be fasting. They were simply going through the motion, and the Lord made it clear that kind of fasting does not impress Him. Their purpose of fasting was not to devote time to God but to gain a blessing.

[6] "No, this is the kind of fasting I want: Free those who are wrongly imprisoned; lighten the burden of those who work for you. Let the oppressed go free and remove the chains that bind people. [7] Share your food with the hungry and give shelter to the homeless. Give clothes to those who need them, and do not hide from relatives who need your help.

In verses 6-7, the Lord explains the kind of fasting that He does want. He wants us to be willing to lay down our lives for others. To lighten the burden of those who work for you, remove the chains that bind people, feed the hungry, give shelter to the homeless, and give to those who are in need. Do not hide from those in need. In verses 8-9, I want to show the NKJV as well.

[8] "Then your salvation will come like the dawn, and your wounds will quickly heal. Your godliness will lead you forward, and the glory of the Lord will protect you from behind. [9] Then when you call, the Lord will answer. 'Yes, I am here,' he will quickly reply (NLT)

[8] 'Then your light shall break forth like the morning, your healing shall spring forth speedily, And your righteousness shall go before you; The glory of the Lord shall be your rear guard. [9] Then you shall call, and the Lord will answer. You shall cry, and He will say, 'Here I am.' (NKJV)

The Lord explained the kind of fast that moves Him. When you fast in that way, He says He will reply quickly! Your wounds will quickly heal; the Lord will go before you and be your rear guard. Read that again if you must. The Lord explains that He will answer and reply quickly when you fast the way that pleases Him and not for your own selfish reasons. It is time to wake up people. God gives clear instructions in His Word on how to receive answers to your prayers.

"Remove the heavy yoke of oppression. Stop pointing your finger and spreading vicious rumors! [10] Feed the hungry, and help those in trouble. Then your light will shine out from the darkness, and the darkness around you will be as bright as noon.

In verses 9-10, the Lord is basically saying that if the people had put a stop to the tyranny and persecution, pointing their fingers at each other and instead focus on feeding the hungry and helping those in need, then He would answer their prayers. Fasting is not merely refraining from food but also a commitment to justice and the poor.

What I am about to share really surprised me, and it will most likely surprise you too. Notice that God did not mention one time in Isaiah 58 that this kind of fast is abstaining from food. We learn throughout Scripture in the Old Testament as well as the New Testament that there is indeed a time for a fast where we abstain from food. But this fast the Lord is talking about in Isaiah 58 is living a fasted life. And that is what I hope for all of you.

God is looking for those who are willing to lay their lives down for others. To be the kind of person that gives or serves even when they themselves are in need. God is looking to see if we are conforming to His image. He is not interested in the motion if your heart's not in the right place. We are called to serve. Not occasionally or once a year during the Holidays. We are called to be living sacrifices in order to emulate Jesus Christ Himself.

Luke 6:38 says,

"Give, and it will be given to you: good measure, pressed down, shaken together and running over will be put into your bosom. For with the same measure that you use, it will be measured back to you."

God is saying when you give to others, I will give to you. When you help others, I will help you. Tell God right now, God, I am coming after you with all my heart. Show me, Lord, if my heart is not in the right place. Help me to conform to Your image. Teach me, Lord, to live an authentic, fasted life. Amen.

Sometime after the Lord revealed His heart to me in Isaiah 58, I had an opportunity to live out the kind of fast Jesus talks about in Isaiah 58. Below is a personal testimony.

Providing A Home for The Homeless

The testimony I am about to share is something I went through personally. To be clear, I am not sharing this testimony to receive accolades from men. I am sharing this now to show you that fasting is not only about abstaining from food. Living a sacrificial life or a fasted life goes much deeper. A friend of mine had a family member who had just accepted Jesus into his heart. This man had been homeless for years as well as his 2-year-old son.

It was my understanding this man was looking for a chance to get back on his feet, find a job and provide a home for him and his little boy. I was not in a position to provide for them financially, but I offered what I had. And that was a bed, clean blankets, food, and a warm shower. My son and I talked it over, prayed about it quickly, and decided to help this family out short-term. In the days following, I came across a verse in Isaiah 58. ***Isaiah 58:7** says, "Share your food with the hungry, and give shelter to the homeless. Give clothes to those who need them, and do not hide from relatives who need your help."*

I felt we were answering a call from God. The first day our guest arrived with his son, he had tears in his eyes, hardly believing what was happening. The first week they were with us, my heart was full. Knowing that neither the dad nor son had slept in a real bed for a long time broke my heart, but I was thankful we had a bed for them with fresh, clean linens. Seeing the two of them snuggled up together, sleeping soundly, put a smile on my face.

Watching Dad and his son play in our pool together while laughing made me feel like everything was going to be alright. Making them homemade meals that the little two-year-old had never tried before was fulfilling. He quickly fell in love with sloppy joes and waffles. There were also moments that broke my heart. Finding out that this little guy most likely never had his teeth brushed until now was heart-breaking. Or that he wet the bed every night because he was never properly potty trained. But the most heart-breaking for me was witnessing how desperate he was for love and attention. I hope that while they were staying with us that there were some God seeds planted in their lives.

Living a fasted life and having a servant attitude will not always be convenient. We may be in need ourselves, but if you read God's Word, He does not suggest that we only help when it's convenient. Neither does He tell us only to give when we have an abundant supply. So even though I had my own concerns, I trusted God to provide for all of us, and He did. God promises that when you seek Him diligently and are willing to serve others, He will guide you continually. When you seek Him with all your heart and soul, serve others with sincerity, then He promises that He will strengthen you and your health. Going through the motions is not enough. Making excuses that you are too busy will not cut it.

Chapter Seventeen

Fasting will Help You Find God's Will for Your Life

For the past few years, I had this unsettling stirring in my spirit. It's hard to explain it, and when I did try to explain it to others, I did not feel like anyone truly understood me. In all honesty, I did not understand it myself. Later, I learned that God put that intense stirring in my spirit.

For the most part, I had accomplished almost everything I put my little heart too. I was led into a career that I became very passionate about. Even though being a realtor was not something I had thought about, it sort of fell into my lap. I received my bachelor's degree while working full-time and being a single parent to a baby. What really motivated me to finish college was something my grandmother had said to me. When she found out I was pregnant, she suggested that I would not finish college because I was having a baby. That stirred something up inside of me.

I thought to myself, not only am I going to get my degree, but I will get 4.0's and make the Dean's list. Boy, was I out to show her. That is exactly what I did. I made the Dean's list and graduated. Throughout thc ycars, my life was busy. Raising a son, working full time, sports, Youth Group, teaching Bible study, attending Christian retreats, well, you get the picture. Fast forward many years, I finally bought my own condo, opened my own real estate company, and opened a Concierge company. Even though I had accomplished a lot, I had this strong feeling that there was more. But I did not know what that more was. The stirring in my spirit was so strong that I felt like I was going to explode from the inside out. I remember thinking, is this really all there is? We wake up, get our kids to school, go to work, pick up kids from school, attend sporting events, grocery shop, cook, pay bills and we do all over again.

Don't get me wrong, all of what I mentioned are blessings. We have responsibilities we need to attend to, and raising our kids is one of the greatest blessings of all. But I thought there is no way this is all there is to life. As time went on and I was not getting answers from God, the stirring in my spirit became almost unbearable. Sometimes, I felt upset with God because this feeling was so intense, yet I was not feeling like I was getting answers from Him. A few times, I had cried out to God in desperation and told Him if this is all there is to life, I would rather He take me home now. Not because my life was horrible, it was far from horrible. On the contrary, I have lived a very blessed and happy life so far.

I have an amazing family, I have been truly blessed to be a mother to a wonderful son, my friends are a blessing, I have had success and failure. It has not always been easy, but God has carried me through the hard times along with the support and encouragement from my family. I did not even feel this void in my life that so many do because they are searching for something to belong to. I am never bored and do not get lonely, so it was not from that. I remember praying to God and letting Him know that if He is going to keep me here on earth, then I want more. In other words, I was not going to settle for a life of the daily grind and the same daily rituals. I needed more! Even though I did not know what that more was yet.

One day I was listening to one of my favorite pastors, Matt Gibson, with Rainmakers Ministries in Traverse City, MI. His teaching spoke to me. One of the things he spoke about was our busy lifestyles. We keep ourselves so busy and often tell God we would spend more time with Him when we are not working 60+ hours a week. God may put it on our hearts to pray about something, and we may have the thought that we will pray after we finish cleaning up the dishes. The problem is most of us will not make the time, and when we do, it's a quick short prayer. The other thing that my pastor touched on was when Jesus spoke to the many churches about their works in the book of Revelation.

Jesus did not say to the churches, I know your heart. He did not come to the churches and say, I know your intentions. What Jesus was demonstrating was that He looks at the fruit to inspect the tree. Or He is looking at the lampstand to see if it's bearing light. Light always involves the removal of darkness with regard to biblical history. The importance of light is spoken of in the beginning of Genesis. Genesis 1:2 says, *"the earth was without form, and void; and darkness was on the face of the deep. And the Spirit of God was hovering over the face of the waters. Then God said, "Let there be light!"* God spoke, and light came into being. Light symbolizes the holy God, the presence of God, and God's favor. God is light and the Father of lights, who dispels darkness. In John 8, Jesus declares that He is the light of the world.

When we are born again, we leave behind the old life in darkness and live our new life in the light of Christ Jesus. Although Satan can disguise himself as an angel of light, believers in Christ Jesus live in the true light of salvation, laying aside the old deeds of darkness. Ephesians 5:8-11 says, *"For you were once darkness, but now you are light in the Lord. Walk as children of light (for the fruit of the Spirit is in all goodness, righteousness, and truth), finding out what is acceptable to the Lord. And have no fellowship with the unfruitful works of darkness, but rather expose them."*

God knows everything. He knows what is in your heart, and He knows your motives. He knows your every thought; therefore, you cannot deceive Him. God is looking at your lampstand to see if it's bearing light. In the Bible, James is the one who teaches that we are saved by grace through faith, but he is also the one that says he will show us his faith by his works. In other words, James was saying that he is not going to talk about being a believer, but he is going to live out being a believer. The fact that Jesus makes these statements to the churches, I know your works, means that He is expecting us to live out what we believe.

It is not enough for us to say we believe. Our beliefs must be enough to drive us to action. So how do we know if it's driving us to action? I strongly suggest taking some time to examine your life thoroughly. This teaching had me reflecting on my busy schedule. I have been so self-consumed with my responsibilities that I was not making time to reach out to others who may need help or encouragement. I realized that this was part of what the more to life is about that I was asking God about. That stirring in my spirit was God teaching me how to live a fasted life.

A while ago, I completed what I called "My 40-Day Transformation Journey." Part of this journey was for the purpose of doing things to better myself. Including getting back onto a schedule of waking up at 4:30 am to spend time alone with God. I also wanted to get back on a consistent workout schedule to better my health. And lastly, I have had questions for God that I have been praying about for many years but did not feel up to this point that I had received definite answers. I was eager to find out what God's plan was for this next chapter of my life.

I also wanted to know what the story was behind that intense stirring in my spirit. I went into this transformation journey expecting to hear from the Lord. One day while on a walk, I was listening to a teaching from one of my favorite teachers, and what he said really struck a chord with me. I ended up listening to that video four times that day. What he said was, **"God is more interested in having a relationship with you than He is in what you can do for Him."** When I heard those words, I had to rewind it and listened to it several times. I was on a trail where there were other people, and most of the time, when I am on my walks, I end up talking to people. I was hoping no one would stop to talk to me because I had tears rolling down my cheeks as I listened intently to the message. I knew God was speaking to me, and this was a significant revelation in my life. God's will for all our lives is to have an intimate relationship with Him. That message was powerful, because, I felt a heavy weight had been lifted off of my shoulders.

Another revelation that occurred during this journey happened while in prayer. While in prayer one day, I felt the Lord ask me what were some of the happiest events during my childhood. I had a lot of them, but when I narrowed it down, I remembered certain events, and I felt the Lord stop me there. A few of my happiest moments were when I volunteered for the Special Olympics and any time I was at a Christian retreat. I knew at that moment I would be hosting Christian retreats. I believe, God also showed me the property that I will one day own and will be able to hold Christian retreats at. It is something I have wanted to do, but because I have been so busy, I forgot about it. I am sharing all of this with you because I want you to see that you will get answers when you take the time to listen to God. God has a purpose for your life, and I feel that too many people just drift through life. If you have had that feeling that there must be more to life than what you are doing, then earnestly seek the Lord. Chances are, He is the One that has put that upon your heart. God has a path for each of us and it's up to us to seek God to find out what He has pre-ordained for us.

Chapter Eighteen

Get Creative with Your Fast

During one of my more recent fasts, I thought: if fasting is that powerful, then why are we all not fasting every day? As I began to seek the Lord about this, I came across other believers where God had spoken to them also about being creative with their time of fasting. There are several ways we can incorporate fasting into our daily lives. We do not have to stick to the typical 3-day, 7-day, 14-day, 21-day, or 40-day fasts. Here are some ways you can incorporate fasting so it can become a part of your learning to live a fasted lifestyle.

1. Fast one meal a day for a specified amount of time
2. Fast two meals a day for a specified amount of time
3. Fast solid foods only for a specified amount of time
4. Drink water only for a specified amount of time
5. Eat fruits and vegetables only for a specified amount of time

As you begin to practice the discipline of fasting and prayer, you will hear God more clearly when He calls you to fast something specific for a specified amount of time. Keep a journal and write down what you feel the Lord spoke to you during your time of fasting and prayer. Even if it does not seem relevant now, write it down because it may make sense to you later on. You may not understand what God is trying to show you right now, but if it is from Him, He will reveal it to you and give you understanding. On so many occasions during my prayer time, the Lord will put a journal on my mind that I wrote a while ago, and when I go back to read it, there was an answer in that journal just waiting for me. It's important to understand that sometimes a breakthrough does not happen right away. From my own experience, the breakthrough usually happens after I have completed a fast.

Fasting does not have to be boring. Our God is a creative God, and it's alright to get creative with your time of fasting. Some of the creative ways I have incorporated fasting into my busy lifestyle are mentioned below.

- If I have a busy schedule one month, I may dedicate an hour every Thursday during my lunch hour.
- Some weeks I may fast breakfast every day that week.
- Block out a weekend. At times I will block an entire weekend off to devote to fasting and prayer. While on a walk I may listen to the Bible app, one of my favorite pastors or just pray.
- Evening fasts. Sometimes I will block time off usually from 6:00 pm – 10:00 pm. Rather than spending the evening watching television I lock myself in my bedroom. I let my son know what I am doing so he knows not to interrupt unless it's an emergency.
- Unplanned prayer times. This is not a fast but there are occasions where I feel that I need to stop what I am doing and spend time in prayer. I go into my room with my phone shut off and my door closed. Sometimes, I may be in there for an hour or a few hours. The unplanned prayer times are some of my favorite moments. I have learned it's usually a prompting from the Holy Spirit. And the revelations I receive are inspiring.

The majority of my time spent in fasting is solely for the purpose of drawing closer to God. However, there are times I fast for a specific breakthrough. When I'm fasting for a particular situation, I prefer to block off a certain amount of time. Our schedules are busy and we all have a lot of responsibilities so it's not always feasible to block off a large amount of time. Which is why I feel God will honor our creative times of fasting and prayer.

Chapter Nineteen

Preparing for a Fast & Ending a Fast

If you are new to fasting, it's important to start slow, especially if you are doing a liquid-only fast. You want to allow your body to get accustomed to the drop in food intake. Start by fasting one meal a day or one day a week. If you have never fasted before, I would not recommend you do a 21-day liquid-only fast your first time. Fasting takes discipline and commitment, and the last thing you want to do is set yourself up for failure before you begin. If God has called you to do a fast, I would be obedient to whatever He calls you to do.

From my own experience, I can tell you trying to do a 21-day fast my first few times was not the right choice for me. Not only did I not make it through the full 21 days, but then I felt like I failed myself and God. I know now that God was not upset with me for not completing the full 21 days. On the contrary, He honored the fact that I was seeking after Him. Remember, God is more interested in having a relationship with you than He is in the Christian disciplines or what you can do for Him. Those eventually come naturally, as you draw closer to God, and He puts His desires on your heart.

Before the Fast

If you are planning on an extended fast, start preparing one week or a few days before the actual fast. Start by cutting down on food intake, eat smaller meals, drink a lot of water, begin to cut out sweet drinks and heavy foods. What has worked for me is cutting out foods such as pasta, breads, and potatoes a week before I start my fast. I load up on fruits and vegetables and will eat lighter meals.

During the Fast

Spend the time that you would normally use for preparing meals to pray and seek the Lord. Keep a journal on why you are fasting and what the Lord is speaking to you during the fast. Drink plenty of water. The first few days are the most challenging but don't give up. When your stomach begins to feel hunger pains, pray! Ask the Lord to give you strength. If you feel light-headed, try adding some lemon to your water. In the evenings or on cold days I add lemon to hot water. Buy the gallon water jugs and carry it with you throughout your day.

Ending the Fast

Whatever you do, do not break your fast by eating a greasy cheeseburger or heavy foods. I made the biggest mistake by coming off a 3-day fast one time by eating Velveeta Macaroni and Cheese. I don't even eat that stuff but when I am fasting sometimes, I crave foods that I rarely eat. I was sick for hours because I did not take the advice to break from my fast slowly. It's best to end your fast by eating lighter foods and smaller portions throughout the day. You may need to do this for 1-3 days after your fast. It takes me about two days before I can go back to my normal eating routines. I recommend eating light foods at least for the first day off your fast, such as soup, salads, vegetables, and fruit.

Chapter Twenty

The Six "P" Checklist for Fasting

Here is a checklist that I put together to help you prepare and position yourself to receive from the Lord during your times of prayer and fasting.

1. Prepare

You can start preparing for your fast days ahead of time. Begin to pray about your fast days before. This will help you to prepare yourself mentally. Plan to block off some time if you can. Schedule a babysitter if you need one. If you are doing a fast on a work day, be sure to pack enough water to get you through the day.

2. Purpose

Decide the purpose for your fast. Write your purpose down in a journal along with Bible promises that cover your situation. Meditate on those Scripture verses and ask the Lord for understanding and to open your spiritual eyes and ears.

3. Proclaim

Proclaim the purpose of your fast to the Lord.

4. Presume

Presume that even before you begin your fast that what you are believing for, you are going to receive it.

5. Pray

Use this time to pray and seek the Lord.

6. Praise

The Bible tells us that God is enthroned or inhabits the praises of His people. When God is enthroned, things happen. He gives us peace and rest when we praise Him, so let God hear your praise and thanksgiving.

Chapter Twenty-One

Salvation Prayer

Choosing to receive Jesus Christ as your Lord and Savior is one of the most important decisions you ever will make. You can say a simple prayer such as the one below or reach out to one of your local churches to meet with a pastor.

Romans 10:9-13 says,

> [9] *that if you confess with your mouth the Lord Jesus and believe in your heart that God has raised Him from the dead, you will be saved.* [10] *For with the heart one believes unto righteousness, and with the mouth confession is made unto salvation.* [11] *For the Scripture says, "Whoever believes on Him will not be put to shame."* [12] *For there is no distinction between Jew and Greek, for the same Lord over all is rich to all who call upon Him.* [13] *For "whoever calls on the name of the Lord shall be saved.*

John 3:3 says,

> [3] *Jesus answered and said to him, "Most assuredly, I say to you, unless one is born again, he cannot see the kingdom of God."*

The salvation prayer is not a specific set of words, and the following is merely a guideline. You are acknowledging in your heart and confessing with your mouth that Jesus is Lord, believing that Jesus died for all your sins and was raised three days later, followed by repenting of your sins and getting baptized in the name of Jesus.

Pray out loud, *Jesus I confess that You are my Lord and Savior. I believe in my heart that You died for my sins and that God raised You from the dead. I admit that I am a sinner. Today I repent of my sins and ask You to forgive me of all of my sins through Your Son Jesus Christ. From this day forward, help me to live every day for You and in a way that pleases You. Come into my life now, Lord. By faith, in Your word, I receive salvation now. Thank You for saving me! Amen.*

If you just received Jesus as your Lord and Savior, you are now born again, and the truth of God's Word instantly comes to pass in your spirit. The next step is to get baptized. You can do this by reaching out to one of your local pastors.

Chapter Twenty-Two

Personal Testimonies

Although I have already shared several personal testimonies throughout this book, I thought I would share with you a few others that have impacted my life. In my opinion, sharing our personal testimonies of how God has worked in our lives can be a source of encouragement for others. Up until now, I have not shared my story or testimonies with a lot of people. There are very few that know my story but God has been working on my heart to start sharing. The last few testimonies I share in this book are for the purpose of showing you how God can work on our behalf if we let Him.

The Home on the Lake

It was a cold January day when I began to look for a new home for my son and me. My ex and I were in the middle of a divorce, and living in the same home was no longer an option. Being a real estate agent, I did not expect to have a hard time finding a home. As it turned out, it was a lot harder than I anticipated. I spent many hours a day looking up homes online and then previewing them in person. There were many days when I came home in tears. I recall one day in particular. It was a Monday afternoon when I arrived home right before my son got off the school bus. I cried so hard when I got home because I was mentally and physically exhausted trying to find a home for my son and me. But I had to quickly pull myself together so my son would not know that I had just been crying. Sometime later in the day, I read something that said, let go and let God. That night while I was in prayer, I said, alright Lord, I will let go of this and let You handle this for me. You know we need to move out fast as we no longer feel safe here. I am praying for a safe home for my son and me. Lord, I have no idea what that perfect home looks like or where it is, but I trust that You have the perfect place for us.

I committed not to fret over this anymore and would not allow myself to spend entire days searching for a home. My plan was to allow myself ten minutes in the morning to look up homes, and then I would be done for the day. That night I felt peace as I handed over my burden to the Lord. The following morning after I got my son on the school bus, I logged onto Craigslist at 8:03 AM. A new listing was posted at 7:59 AM. A 3-bedroom, 2 bath home with 170' of private frontage on a beautiful lake. Approximately 2,700 square foot home with two fireplaces, large back deck, and a private dock for $800/month. I nearly passed out.

Immediately, I sent an email. By mid-afternoon, I had not heard back from the owner. On my way home, I decided to drive around this lake looking for a For Rent sign but no luck. After I arrived home, I began to make dinner but left my laptop open on the kitchen counter so I could see when this person had responded to me. The email finally came through. The man told me the home was still available and it was mine if I wanted it. He explained that he and his wife bought the house the year before; however, they were transferred over to Africa for a missionary trip that could keep them there for 1-5 years.

He said they were looking for someone who would take good care of their home, and money was not as important to them as having someone responsible in their home. Which was the reason they were renting it out for only $800.00 a month. This waterfront home would normally rent for at least three times that. I was so excited as my son and I looked at the pictures of the home repeatedly. I was nearly in tears, hardly believing what was going on. Yet, very thankful that God had answered my prayer. That moment of happiness did not last long though. I had emailed my application to the guy and right away he asked me to wire him the deposit.

Immediately, I knew this was a scam because only scammers ask you to wire money. I pulled up the tax records, and his name did not match with the name on the tax records. I emailed him back and told him I believe this to be a scam because landlords do not typically ask to have the deposit wired, and secondly, his name was not on the tax records as the owner. I told him I would be contacting the real owner the following morning. He tried to tell me it was not a scam and strongly suggested that I do not contact the man on the tax records.

The following morning, I received a call from a blocked number. It was the guy from the Craigslist ad. This man argued with me for half an hour, trying to convince me that he was the real owner. He even suggested that the guy's name on the tax records would only try to screw my son and me over. I finally said to him, "If you are the rightful owner, then why don't you email me a copy of the deed with your name on it?" He told me he could not do that, because, they had not officially closed on the home yet. And he suggested I wire him the money anyway.

I responded back with, "Do you think I am a fool?" I finally hung up on him and told him I was driving over to the real owner's home to meet with him. Well, he called me back immediately; this time, he forgot to block his number. So, I hung up on him again. In the meantime, I was researching online to try to find the real owner's phone numbers. I was able to find a phone number for the woman who was named on the tax records. I called her office number and left her a message.

I looked in the white pages for the guy's phone number, and there was an address listed but no phone number. I decided to drive to the address listed in the white pages, which was not the same address as the lake house. I introduced myself, told him the story, then showed him the ad on Craigslist and asked him if it was a scam. He told me that it was a scam. I let him know that I was on my way to report it to the police, gave him my business card, and said, if you are interested in renting your home, give me a call, and obviously, I know $800 a month is too low so let me know what you'd rent it for.

I headed down to the police station, and they took my report, but there was not much they could do because I never wired the money. However, the detective called this guy directly. Remember he forgot to block his number the last time he called me. She called him and told him that he was to take the ad off Craigslist, and he must never contact me again, or they would consider it harassment, and she would file charges. He hung up on her. As I was on my way home, I received a call from the ex-wife of the real owner of this home.

She could hardly believe my story, but she shared with me that she heard the house was going back to the bank. It is such a small world; she asked me if I knew so and so. I chuckled and said, he is my soon-to-be ex-husband. Apparently, she had gone to high school with my ex. A few minutes later, I received a call from the owner of the home. He told me he was interested in renting the home, but it's complicated. He explained that his house was up for sale, it had been vacant for about a year, and it may be going back to the bank. However, he was going to try to sell it during the 6-month redemption period.

In other words, if I moved in and a buyer came along, I could potentially have to move out in 30 days. Then, of course, there was a chance that it would not sell during the 6-months redemption period, and I would have a temporary place to stay for at least six months. I was a little uneasy with it all, but I also had a feeling it could all work out. So, I let him know that I was interested but inquired about what the rent would be. I was certain he would be asking a lot more than $800 a month because it was a beautiful home on a lake with private water frontage.

He told me that with all the uncertainty and the high heating cost in the winter, he would only charge me $700 a month. My jaw dropped; I was shocked and excited. We decided to meet at the house right away. I arrived at the home and could see that the driveway had not been plowed so I had to park at the top of the driveway. I trudged through two feet of snow in the middle of February. As I entered through the front door, I immediately saw the frozen lake through the living room windows. The windows may have been covered with frost and the home was chilly because it sat vacant for a year, but I was already in love. I knew I could make this place a warm, cozy home for my son and me. The owner explained that I was also doing him a favor.

Because the home was in the six-month redemption period, the bank would be stopping by any day to see if the home was vacant or occupied. In Michigan, the law is that if the home is occupied, then the owners have six months to redeem it or sell it. If the home is vacant, then the owners have 30 days. In this case, time was of the essence because the bank was planning to stop by in the next day or two. The owner and I agreed that he would turn everything on for me right away, and I would start moving in the following day. As we were leaving the home that night, another couple showed up. This couple had also seen the home on Craigslist. The owner and I decided not to share with them that I was renting the home.

We just explained to them that it was a scam. When I got home that evening, I posted an ad on Craigslist about this home and explained that the first ad was a scam and warned everyone not to wire money to the scammer. Because of my ad, I had received several emails thanking me for making everyone aware and reporting him. A few people shared with me that this was their dream home. I understood because it was nearly everything I had ever wanted in a home as well. However, because of how sad some people were, I chose not to share with any of them that I had met the real owner and would soon be renting the home.

I was thankful that the other interested parties were not realtors, so they did not think to check the tax records to locate the real owners of the home. During the six months, we had several showings on the home; thankfully, no one bought it. I had put over $3000 into the home with regards to some upgrades and repairs. May came around, and the homeowner informed me that he and the bank had agreed to a deed-in-lieu of foreclosure. This meant that the bank would be getting the home back a lot sooner than the 6-month redemption period.

The bank would own the home within 30 days rather than at the end of the six months. The owner gave me a 30-day notice and apologized. I was not happy because that meant I had to find us a new home within 30 days. I am the queen of research, so naturally, I began to research what a tenant's rights were in a situation such as this. I found out that by law, that the bank had to offer me at least 90 days or offer me cash for keys. I put two and two together and felt that the homeowner's attorney and the bank's attorney had suggested that the owner provide me with a written 30-day notice, so the bank did not have to offer me any of the options I mentioned above.

After learning this, I decided to wait for the bank to contact me with the next step. I informed the owner of what I found out, and he did confirm what I had suspected. His attorney and the bank's attorney suggested that he give me written notice, so the bank did not have to offer me anything. At this point, I was grateful for my experience and knowledge as a realtor but also for the fact that I research everything. A month later, the owner of the home called me asking me where June rent was. I reminded him that he gave me a 30-day notice and that, at this point, the home should be the bank's responsibility.

He then explained to me that the bank had messed up some paperwork which now requires him and the bank to start the process all over with regards to the deed in lieu of foreclosure. I told the owner I need time to think about this and will reach out to him later in the day. I emailed him later and mentioned that I have no problem paying him that month's rent, but I would need something in writing from him that stated the 30-day notice was null and void. I also suggested that if we were going to continue with the lease, I needed a few repairs completed. I did not hear back from him for over a week.

I finally texted him one day, and his response was, I am still digesting your email and trying to figure out what's going on with the bank. As it turned out, the deed-in-lieu of foreclosure was going to take a little longer. All in all, he completed the repairs I requested, and we continued with the terms of the lease in place. My son and I had spent a lot of time praying about this house and our current situation. After living in this home for a few months, I realized that this home was everything I had wanted in a home since I was a little girl. I had always dreamed of living in a brick house on the lake.

A home that had a massive fireplace on each floor, a covered front porch to sit outside on during the rainfalls, a large back deck to enjoy the view of the lake and the sun, a yard with little to no maintenance, and a large master bedroom with an extra-large walk-in closet. After pulling up the plat map for our property, I realized that this lot was the largest lot on our road with the most private water frontage. In our opinion, we had the best views of the lake. September came around, and I received notice that the home was now banked owned and to no longer pay the previous home owner rent money.

The owner came over a day later to fix something on the thermostat, and I mentioned that I was sorry to hear that the deed-in-lieu of foreclosure did not work out. He said to me, "What are you talking about? I am signing the deed-in-lieu of foreclose today and handing the keys over to the bank." The bank did not realize that the home was not going into foreclosure. Their original notice in the newspaper had missing information, which legally made the notice null and void. And the bank (Fannie Mae) did not realize that the owner was signing a deed-in-lieu of foreclosure, with the original bank owner, Huntington Bank. This would be the bank that the owner had a mortgage with.

It was complicated for sure. At this point, I reached out to the Realtor hired by Fannie Mae to post the notice on the front door of the pre-closure process. We spoke about what my possible options might be. He informed me that in his 30 years in business, the banks do not rent out banked-owned homes. And even if I were interested in purchasing the house, the bank would still require me by law to move everything out and then move back in once the home was purchased. I was now down to a couple of weeks, if that. Once the bank realized that I was not planning to move out that quickly, they requested a copy of my previous lease, my letter of intent to buy the home, and a pre-qualification letter from the bank, all of which I gladly provided. In the meantime, I received a package in the mail from a property management company stating that I must get in touch with them as soon as possible. I called them right away, and we played phone tag for a few days. A few days later, the bank's Realtor called me to discuss my next steps with Fannie Mae. I was mainly discussing a purchase price. He asked me if I had a price in mind. I did, but I did not want to tell him what it was. He suggested I start at $150,000. I asked him to repeat what he said, and he said $150,000. This was the number I had in mind all along. Even though, at one point, this home was worth half a million. I had mentioned to the Realtor that a property management company had also been in touch with me, and he had no information on this.

A few days later, Fannie Mae's property management company and I finally spoke. They asked me for a copy of the lease I had with the previous owner. This property management company offered me three options. 1) Cash for keys to move out. 2) Continue with the lease terms I had with the previous owner, which would only be good for another month. 3) Start a new lease at a different price with Fannie Mae, which could be a year-long lease. At this point, I was more interested in a year-long lease, but I was a little worried about the rental market price.

The property management company came back with a rent price of $650 a month. They would take care of the taxes and insurance, and all repairs. They offered me a month-to-month or a one-year lease. I chose the one-year lease. Because I provided a letter of intent to purchase this home, they informed me they would not put the house up for sale during this time or market the home for sale. When I was ready to purchase the home, they told me to inform them, and they would then change my lease to a month-to-month lease. You can imagine how blown away I was with all of this working out to my advantage.

A few weeks later, I reached out to the bank's Realtor to let him know I signed a year lease and would be writing up an offer on the home probably near the end of the lease. To my surprise, he informed me that there was already an offer on the house a while back. Apparently, the bank or the property management company never told him of our agreement. The offer he received was now null and void because I had a contract in place with the bank and the property management company and I had first right of refusal and a one-year lease in place.

About six months into my lease, the property management company informed me to stop making payments. I refused to stop making payments because I was afraid this would look negligent on my part. But the property management company explained to me that Fannie Mae no longer owned the home and that they were forcing the previous bank, Huntington Bank to buy the house back due to some deficiency in paperwork. I had no idea what that entailed, and now I had no idea who even owned the home. I have never seen anything like this before. I reached out to Huntington Bank, and they had no idea what is going on.

I explained to the guy at Huntington Bank that because of some deficiency in the paperwork that Fannie Mae would be forcing Huntington bank to repurchase the home. The guy at Huntington bank was clueless. This left me with no one to talk to and zero idea of who the home belonged to now. That kind of uncertainty left a lot of room for anxiety, but I chose to put my trust in the Lord. Months later, I received an email from the REO department of Huntington Bank. They informed me that they did not have a rental management company. Therefore, they had no legal way to lease the home back to me until I was ready to purchase the home. Now my only choice was to purchase the home at twice the rate I could have bought it for when Fannie Mae owned it or move out.

A so-called friend offered to purchase the home for me, and offered me a lease-back back until I was ready to purchase the home from him. I do not wish to share that part of the story because I don't want to talk bad about this person. But let's say he ended up not being a friend, and was not truthful in his ability to get financing for the home. I could not purchase the home and we ended up moving out nine months later. One good thing about this nine-month period was that I lived in the home at no cost for nine months.

Looking back now, God had provided a way for me to purchase this home early on for way less than what the home was worth. I was afraid to make a move that quickly, but had I trusted God I would have had a nice investment in my portfolio. The blessings that came from living in this home were abundant. The friends that my son and I made during the years living there ended up being life-long friends. I hosted Christian weekend retreats at this home, and many were baptized in the lake. This home also served as a place for friends to live when they were in-between places. And this home served as a place of healing for my son and me after my divorce.

My Brand-New SUV Testimony

One especially important lesson I have learned is to never make big purchases without first praying about it. And certainly, do not make big purchases in desperation or in a hurry. Years ago, I had purchased a 2010 Dodge Journey in desperation and in a hurry. I have a journal of this experience, and the pages are many. It could easily be a book itself. The problems I had with this vehicle started the very night I purchased the Dodge Journey, and the problems continued the entire time I had it. After years of consistent problems, along with the money this vehicle was costing me, I knew I had to get rid of it and purchase another vehicle.

Because of this experience, I was concerned with purchasing another used vehicle. I spent about two years praying about what to do before calling my friend, Mark Soper, who works for a local dealership in Traverse City, Michigan. My credit was not great because I did not have any recent credit, so Mark suggested I open a few credit cards to establish more recent credit, and then we could revisit car buying in six months. Reluctantly, I opened a few credit cards. A few months later, I stopped by the dealership to get some maintenance done on the Dodge Journey, and Mark asked me if I had opened those credit cards he recommended. I told him that I had, but I had not used them yet. He laughed at me and explained that I needed to use them to make a difference in my credit report. I don't like credit cards after I got myself into trouble with them in my early 20's so naturally, I was afraid to use them. My first charge on one of my credit cards was an oil change while I was at the dealership that day.

I spent the next few months praying and asking the Lord to show me what to do because I knew the Dodge Journey would not last much longer. It had been months since I last spoke with Mark. Then, one day while I was in the middle of working on my new business venture, I suddenly had this thought that I was to reach out to Mark. I sent him a quick email, and to my surprise, he responded immediately, and we set an appointment to meet that very day. I had a few real estate closings that morning but was able to meet with him right afterward.

I walked into the dealership thinking we were going to discuss what my future options would be. He had other plans. When I arrived at the dealership, I didn't even have a chance to sit down. He took me straight to a brand-new vehicle to test drive. We walked over to this brand-new SUV, and my first thought was how beautiful it was, and I figured it would be a fun test drive, but there was no way I could afford something like this. This vehicle only had 40 miles on it. After the test drive, we returned to the shop, and Mark immediately began the paperwork.

I thought he was looking up different options; I had no idea he was working on the paperwork for me to purchase this vehicle. The guys at the shop took my Dodge Journey in the back to inspect it so they could give me a trade-in value. Thankfully, I just had two real estate closings that morning and made the deposits right before I met with Mark, which allowed me a nice down payment on my new SUV. One of the offers the dealership had going on at this time was $10,000 off the Hyundai's, which worked out to my advantage because I was still owed $9,800 on the Dodge Journey.

Which is another reason Mark chose to show me the Hyundai. The next thing I knew, I was approved for this brand-new vehicle. Now I had to decide whether I wanted to go forward with this purchase right now or think about it over the weekend. I had been praying diligently about this for months. And because I had felt it was the Lord that put it on my heart to reach out to my friend at that very moment and had peace about this, I decided it was better to move on this right now. I was confident God was leading me and had His hand in all of this.

I mentioned earlier that one of the lessons I have learned is to never make big purchases in a hurry or without praying. I had been praying that God provided a way for me to get rid of the Dodge and purchase a new vehicle for a long time. So, this was not an impulsive purchase. With the lake house situation, I also learned that when God provides a way, sometimes it's important not to wait too long as I did with the house. It was a Friday night around 5:00 pm when I left the dealership and drove off in a brand new 2017 Hyundai Santa Fe Sport with Turbo.

I could not believe that just happened. That was not planned. I thought I was only going in to talk with Mark and discuss some future options. A month later, I ran into Mark at my high school reunion and asked him what they did with that Dodge Journey. And this is how I knew that God had His hand in this all along, and I am so grateful I listened to Him and moved when He told me to move. Mark said to me that the Dodge Journey sat in the parking lot all weekend, exactly where it was left after the guys inspected it. On Monday, when the guys got to work, they attempted to drive it into the shop to clean it and get it ready to sell. The minute they turned it on, the engine blew. Just like that, it was all over for that Dodge Journey. Had I decided to "think" more about the decision, I would have been in trouble.

The thought had crossed my mind to take the weekend to think and pray about it. But something inside me said you have been praying about this long enough. It's time to make a move. Had I not messaged Mark that day, I would have been in trouble. Had Mark not messaged me back that very day, I would have been in trouble. Because I was only going to purchase a vehicle through him, had he not been in that day, things would have gone bad for me. Had I driven the Dodge Journey home that Friday night, the engine would have blown on my way out of the dealership parking lot. I would have been stuck with a vehicle that had no engine and still owed about $9,800 on it.

God KNEW all of this ahead of time. He knew the engine was going to go. He knew it would happen that Friday on my way home. He knew Mark would be in the office that day, and He knew the deal they were offering on the Hyundai's that month would be to my advantage. I told Mark I felt bad that it happened, but he told me it was not my problem anymore. He said the manager was upset that the trade-in was now worth nothing and even asked who the heck inspected it. Well, I bet that God's hand was in the inspections too.

After hearing that, I knew I made the right choice and knew without a doubt I had God's blessing. A few years after I purchased that vehicle, my sister spoke with Mark about purchasing the same vehicle I have. He told her that it was pretty much impossible, and it would cost her way too much. They no longer had that special going on for that Hyundai.

Book Publishing Testimony

If someone had told me a few years ago that I would be authoring a book, I would have told them they were crazy. Not only did I think I would never have the extra time, but more importantly, the thought of sitting still long enough to write is not something I ever thought I would be able to do. But, to my surprise, here I am today, near ready to get my first book published. This is a testimony of what I went through when I was finally ready to submit my manuscript for editing and publishing.

I have been working on this manuscript since 2018, and in December of 2019, I thought it was finished. I reached out to a book editor that was referred to me by a friend. I spoke with the editor, and the more we spoke, the more excited I got. However, the closer we got to making the commitment to work together, I backed out. Part of the reason was that I was not ready to spend that kind of money yet, but I had a feeling that something wasn't right. I assumed it wasn't the right time. Later I found out that was, in fact, the reason because there was much more that needed to be added to this.

Fast forward a year, and now I was certain my manuscript was ready to submit to a publisher. As you can imagine, I was beyond excited. My mind was racing, and I was calling all my friends and family to share the good news with them that I finished it. It did not take long, though, before the excitement turned to doubt. I began to think about what if it's not good enough or if it's not worthy to be published. This doubt held me back for a month or two before I would move forward with researching publishing companies.

11/1/2020. I wrote a manuscript proposal to send off to a publishing company. It was late in the evening, and I knew I was not providing my best proposal, but I was anxious to send it off to a publisher. This impulsive behavior is something I am still working on. I attached the proposal to my email and clicked on the send button, but it wouldn't send. I tried a few more times, but nothing. The send button in my email always works; this has never happened before. Finally, I closed out my email and opened it again, but the same thing happened. I restarted my computer and tried it again, the same thing. I knew after a dozen tries that this was not what God wanted me to do. I figured maybe He didn't want me to send it that night because it was not a quality proposal, so I figured I would send it in the morning. The following morning, I did not feel peace about sending a proposal to this company, so I left it alone.

11/7/2020. I reached out to a literary agent, but they rejected previewing a proposal because, at the time, they were only working with established authors who could provide them with at least $100,000 royalties. Ok, so I had my first rejection, but this did not stop me.

11/7/2020. I reached out to another publisher, who was close to home, maybe only a few miles from where I live. I thought it would be great to work with a local business. Unfortunately, I never heard back from them.

Now I am suddenly questioning whether this was meant to be published. Maybe God only meant it for me, and this was my journey with Him. I reached out to my mother to ask her if she would briefly read it and give me her honest opinion about whether it should be a published book or blog material. If I chose to share this information in blog format, I would have enough material for a year if I posted once a week.

I emailed my manuscript to my mom, but she did not provide her opinion. She did proofread it for me and assisted with some edits, which I was grateful for. Her strong suit is writing after all. She suggested I send it to a pastor friend of hers because she is biased, which I did. He agreed to read it and said he would gladly give his opinion. He called me immediately after receiving it and told me anything that will draw people to the Lord or to His Word is publish-worthy. He mentioned that he would keep reading the manuscript. However, I never heard from him again. I have no idea if he read the entire manuscript or not.

11/9/2020. I then reached out to one of my Christian mentors back in Michigan, and he agreed to read it and give his honest opinion. Two weeks passed and I did not hear a word from him. So maybe he didn't get the email? I felt for some reason, not to reach out to him to ask him if he received it or had time to preview it briefly. Later, I realized that the email I sent him bounced back. Therefore, he never received the email. I chose not to resend the manuscript to the correct email address.

11/11/2020. One day while talking to my best friend, I shared with her my frustrations and doubts. She offered to preview my manuscript. In fact, she adamantly promised me that she would read it on Thursday on 11/17/2020, on her only day off that week. She promised me repeatedly. Not only did she not read it, but she never responded to any text messages I sent her that day. The text messages I sent her were not related to whether she had time to read it. I never asked her if she had time to read it yet. I know her well and knew if she had been reading it, she would have been contacting me right away. By now, I was feeling like I could not even count on my best friend to keep her word.

However, later in the evening, I knew there was a reason she did not read it. I felt like God did not want her to read it because He did not want me to rely on another person's opinion. I found out the following day my friend ended up taking Benadryl for a rash, and she was knocked out all day. She shared with me after she apologized that she did not respond to one phone call or text the previous day.

11/14/2020. After that, I reached out to another friend from Michigan who is an author. I was hoping he would at least give me his opinion on whether to self-publish or go with traditional publishing. I saw a post from him on social media that he had been out of town for a month. He did reach out to me at the end of the month and gave me his publisher's name and cell phone number. This one sounded promising, and my friend told me if I had any issues getting a hold of his publisher to let him know, and he would reach out to him directly. What this company offered was everything I was looking for. Yet a month went by, and I still had not reached out to him. I cannot explain it. I should have been excited about this opportunity, but something was holding me back from reaching out to this publishing company.

11/15/2020. I reached out to the book editor that I was in contact with the previous year. She helped edit and co-authored my friend's book. I have also referred two of my friends to her in the past year, and they both hired her. She said she would call me the following day between 9:30-11:00 am. For some reason, I had this feeling, though, that she was not the one. I was afraid she would not be able to give me the time I needed to accomplish what I wanted. So, I put that in prayer and trusted that God would direct me. I waited for her call the next day. As it got closer to 11:00 am, I told the Lord that if she cannot keep her commitment to call me between the time she told me she would, I would not hire her. She called me at 10:45 am. A part of me was bummed she called me before 11:00 am because a part of me felt like she wasn't right for this project. But, on the other hand, I was so excited to start with the editing process of my manuscript. Plus, she came highly recommended. In our first conversation, she told me she would be happy to work with me. I did share with her my concerns with why I had been hesitant to self-publish. When I shared with her my goals and expectations, I sensed a bit of hesitation. But from the conversation we had, it sounded like she was excited to take on my project.

11/16/2020. I was lying in bed, and all these ideas came to me about what to say in my book promo video. It was so much that I had to get up and write it all down in my notes on my phone.

11/17/2020. Today I worked on a promo video in PowerPoint. I thought if I could at least get the idea out of my head and into a mockup video, I could move on. And then, I could at least share this idea with my book editor because she said she had connections with people that could do a video for me. I think I began to work on it around 1:00 pm and finished around 6:00 pm. Unfortunately, I was so engrossed in it that I missed a webinar I had registered for. I was getting ready to send the video to my editor and saw an email she sent me at 5:30 pm.

11/17/2020. I received an email from the book editor that after careful consideration and prayer, she and her partner felt that her company would not be a good fit for what I was trying to accomplish. Immediately, I felt rejected.

How could I not feel rejected after having sent my manuscript to several people, only to have no one read it and the fact that the one time I had put a proposal together, my email send button was not working? I was also bothered by the fact that she turned me down, after I had referred two of my friends to her. I thought that maybe God does not want me to publish this, or maybe it's not done yet. I was near tears and spent the next few hours feeling sorry for myself and pouting. My son suggested I be patient and trust that this must not be the right time yet. He told me our timing is not always God's timing. Little did either of know at the time, that he was correct. It would be almost a year later before my manuscript was ready. My son had also just finished watching my mockup video, and he reminded me of the message of my video. We both laughed because he was right. The message I had in the mockup promo video for my book was advice I needed to hear myself at that very moment.

During the past few weeks, I had thoughts that God did not want me to turn to people to get their opinion. I felt as though He was asking me "Why are you not trusting Me?" I felt He was trying to show me that He had given me an assignment that He wanted to bless me and others with, yet I was turning to man to get their opinion. However, I remember reading an article from another author who said sometimes he does let his family and friends read his manuscripts to get their opinion. This was never part of my plan, but after reading that article, I thought, why not.

I finally went to bed around 11:30 pm. But I laid there and was too sad to fall asleep. So, I decided to open the YouTube app on my phone to see if there was anything worth listening to. The minute I opened YouTube, a video appeared that had the headline**, "God says, you weren't rejected, I hid your value from them because they weren't assigned to your destiny."**

I thought, ok Lord, you have my attention! It was an hour-long video. Even though I was tired, I ended up listening to the entire video. God spoke to me through that video, and it was exactly what I needed to hear. So much of what was on that video is also in my book, including fasting and prayer. The next day I listened to the video again and took notes.

11/18/2020. Even though I did not go to bed until 12:30 am, I was woken up at 4:10 am. I felt it was God, and He wanted to speak to me. I went into prayer and felt the Lord tell me to look up Tinsdale Publishing. I had never heard of it and didn't even know if there was one called Tinsdale. So, I googled it, and Tyndale Publishing popped up. I thought this must be the one the Lord was directing me to because I could not find one spelled, Tinsdale. Tyndale is a Christian publishing company. I got excited, but it didn't last long once I began to read through their website. They do not accept unsolicited manuscripts. They only accept proposals from authors they know or maybe one that has a literary agent, and even in that case, they only publish 1% of the manuscripts they receive. Well, shoot, I thought, then why did God bring me here?

Maybe I heard Him wrong, or I just made that name up in my head. I continued to read further down on their website, and they provided a link for authors that do not have a literary agent. It's called ChristianBookProposals.Com. This is where someone like myself can submit a manuscript proposal for $98, and publishers and/or literary agents can reach out to authors directly, or authors can reach out to the publishers and editors listed on this site for a cost. These are publishers looking for unsolicited book proposals in a traditional royalty-based relationship. It allows authors to submit their book proposals in a secure, online format for review by editors from publishing houses that are members of the Evangelical Christian Publishers Association (ECPA). Just to be clear, those that have reached out to me have not been traditional publishers.

I now knew what I was supposed to do. This is the first time I felt peace about it. If only I would learn to be more obedient to what I am feeling in my spirit, I would save myself a lot of grief or the feeling of rejection like I did within the past two weeks. I shared the news with my son this morning, and he said to me, "How could you possibly have gotten an answer that quickly?" He was shocked because he had this feeling that it just wasn't the right time yet for me to publish. I said to him, "What are you talking about? You're the one that gets hired one hour after your job interviews and gets job offers that you never applied for." He laughed. I showed my son a snapshot of the video I watched the night before, and his jaw dropped, and we both began laughing. We were both in awe in the way the Lord chose to speak to me in the last 24 hours. I love all the many ways that God speaks to us.

On 11/18/2020 at 8:48 pm, I submitted my proposal on ChristianBookProposals.com where ECPA members will be able to preview my proposal and contact me directly. I started to work on my book proposal around 1:00-1:30 pm and finished it around 8:30 pm. I felt great peace about this and believed this was indeed the route God wanted me to take. I had never heard of Tyndale Publishing until God spoke the words to me that morning, so I knew this was not from my own doing. The Tyndale Publishing website led me to the Christian Book Proposals website. From there, I would wait for the right publisher to contact me.

1/11/2021. I received my first email from a book publishing company called Advantage Books. I showed my son the email, and I was crying because I knew it was God. I submitted my manuscript to them and had butterflies in my stomach until I heard back from them the following day. To be honest, I was so afraid I would hear it was not what they were looking for. They reached out to me the following day to inform me they were interested in working with me to get my book published. I was beyond excited. The only issue I faced now was that I did not have the extra funds to spend at the moment. I had to trust that God would provide the funds when the time was right. If He wanted it published, He would have to provide a way, or He would have a traditional publisher reach out to me.

1/19/2021. Today I received a contract from Advantage Books to review and sign.

3/4/2021. I finally signed the contract to work with Advantage Books. This was a big step for me on so many levels.

9/17/21. I have been working with the editing team since June. Each day we got closer to finalizing the manuscript the more nervous I got. One night, I had so many thoughts running through my mind that it kept me up nearly all night long. I was feeling so far out of my comfort zone and frankly, quite nervous about putting myself out there. As I prayed about this, I felt the Lord say to me, do you not remember saying to me, is this really all there is? I had a good laugh over that one and was quickly reminded that I asked for this when I told God I wanted more.

I hope that by sharing a few of my personal testimonies with you that it blesses you and encourages you. More importantly, I pray that they encourage you to seek more of God.

Chapter Twenty-Three

Recipes

The recipes I am sharing here were not directed by a doctor and what works from some may not work for others, so please talk to your doctor if you plan on completing an extended fast. I rarely measure or track cooking times. You may need to look up proper measurements and cooking time if you like precision.

Liquid Only Fasts

When I do liquid only fasts I typically only drink lemon water. If I am doing a liquid only fast that lasts longer than 3 days, I will sometimes add in fruit juices, tea, coffee, or chicken broth.

1. Plain water
2. Fruit juices without pulp (Apple, Grape, Cranberry. I water mine down)
3. Broth (Bone, Chicken, Beef, Vegetable, Thai)
4. Tea
5. Coffee (Try to drink your coffee with no sugar or creamer)
6. Make a pitcher of water with your favorite fruit. I use filtered water
    1. Sliced apples and cinnamon sticks
    2. Sliced cucumbers and mint leaves
    3. Sliced oranges
    4. Sliced lemon or lime
    5. Sliced watermelon

Fruit and Vegetable Only Fast

I make all my soups in a crock pot.

Cabbage Soup

In a crock pot add the following ingredients. Cook on high for 4-6 hours.

1. 1 box (32 oz) of your favorite broth
2. 2-4 cups of water
3. Onion chopped
4. Sliced carrots
5. ½ to a full head of cabbage
6. 1-2 cans of diced tomatoes
7. 1 Tbsp of Vegetable Better Than Bouillon

Vegetable Soup

In a crock pot add the following ingredients. Cook on high for 4-6 hours.

1. 1 box (32 oz) of your favorite broth
2. 2-4 cups of water
3. Sliced carrots
4. Sliced celery
5. Diced onion
6. Chopped garlic
7. Kale
8. Spinach
9. Green beans
10. Garbanzo beans

Cucumber & Avocado Salad

Cut cucumber and avocado into bite size squares, add in some cherry tomatoes, red onion, and drizzle balsamic vinegar on top.

Cucumber Onion Salad

Slice cucumbers and onions and place them in a bowl. Add the following ingredients. Let it marinate for a few hours before serving.

1. 1 cup of water
2. ½ cup of distilled white vinegar
3. ¼ cup of olive oil
4. Salt and pepper
5. Pinch of sugar
6. 1-3 cucumbers sliced
7. Sliced onion

Cucumber & Tomato Salad

Slice cucumbers, tomato cut in wedges and diced onion. Drizzle with balsamic vinegar and salt and pepper.

Vegetable Stir Fry

In a pan drizzle oil or vegetable broth, add in garlic and cook for 1-2 minutes, then add in carrots and cook for about 3-5 minutes then add in remaining vegetables; snow peas, peppers, broccoli, and water chestnuts. Buy frozen or already packaged stir fry vegetables for convenience. I stir fry in vegetable broth rather than oil.

Vegetable Kabob

Cherry tomato, red onion, mushrooms, yellow squash, zucchini, bell peppers and pineapple. Grill or bake.

Vegetable Bake

Combine the following ingredients then sprinkle with oil or vegetable broth, garlic salt, salt and pepper. Bake at 350 degrees F for 15-20 minutes.

1. Brussel sprouts halved
2. Asparagus chopped
3. Broccoli
4. Zucchini

Roasted Brussel Sprouts

Preheat the oven to 400 degrees F. Toss Brussel Sprouts with shallots, oil or vegetable broth, salt, and pepper in a medium bowl. Spread on a large, rimmed baking sheet. I use tinfoil on a baking sheet for easy clean up. Roast Brussel sprouts for about 10 minutes. Return to the bowl, toss with vinegar to taste. For added flavor try sprinkling some pomegranate seeds on top or dried cranberries.

Roasted Asparagus

Line the baking sheet and heat the oven to 400 degrees F. Rinse asparagus, drizzle with oil or vegetable broth and garlic salt and bake for about 15-10 minutes.

Roasted Cabbage/Kale/Asparagus

Mix all the vegetables together in a bowl, drizzle oil or vegetable broth and sea salt. Bake at 375 degrees F until done. I usually top this off with feta cheese when I am not fasting

1. ½ head of cabbage rinsed and cut into quarters
2. 1 cup of rinsed kale
3. 1 cup of asparagus rinsed

Strawberry & Apple Salad

1. 1 head of romaine lettuce cut into bite size pieces
2. 1 (10 oz) package of shredded lettuce
3. 1 ½ cup of golden raisins
4. 1 cup of red grapes halved
5. Red onion diced (Approximately ¼ cup or less)
6. 1-2 cups of fresh strawberries
7. 1 cup of your favorite apple
8. Drizzle with strawberry balsamic vinegar

Jen's Homemade Salsa

Dice a few Roma tomatoes (It will depend on how much you are making. I typically only make enough for 1-2 days so I usually dice between 4-6 Roma Tomatoes)

1. Fresh garlic diced
2. Red onion chopped
3. A pinch of fresh cilantro
4. A squeeze of lime
5. Generously sprinkle in sea salt
6. Hot sauce (I use very little, maybe a 1-3 dashes of hot sauce)
7. Add a little bit of oil or vegetable broth

About the Author

Jennifer LaCharite was born and raised in Traverse City, Michigan. It is a beautiful Northern Michigan town that is best known as Cherry Capital of the World and its beautiful freshwater lakes. She lived in Traverse City until her move to Southern California in 2018. Today, Jennifer and her son live in a beautiful beach town in sunny Southern California.

Jennifer graduated college with a Bachelor's Degree in Science. She holds a Broker's license in Michigan and a real estate salesperson license in California. She is the owner and author of Living Fearlessly a Christian website, and as of this book, now an Author of, ***LIVING FEARLESSLY Through Fasting & Prayer***.

When she is not working or writing, she can be found on the golf course or walking the sandy beaches of Southern California. She loves to read, has a passion for learning and a heart for helping others in need.

References

Introduction

1. Revelation 19:16 NKJV
2. Ezekiel 10:14 NKJV

Chapter 1: What Is Biblical Fasting

1. Matthew 3:16 NKJV
2. Matthew 4:1-2 NKJV
3. Matthew 9 NKJV
4. Matthew 11 NKJV
5. Luke 22:35 NIV
6. Matthew 6:16-18 NIV
7. John 6:63 NIV

Chapter 2: What Fasting Is Not

1. "Fast, Fasting" Baker's Evangelical Dictionary of Biblical Theology
2. Luke 18:9-14 NIV

Chapter 3: Different Types of Fasting

1. Matthew 4:1-2 NKJV
2. Deuteronomy 9:9 NKJV
3. Daniel 10:2-3 NKJV
4. Daniel 1:12 NKJV
5. Esther 4:16 NKJV
6. Ezra 8:21 NKJV

Chapter 5: Incentives to Fasting

1. 1 Kings 21:27-29 NKJV
2. Romans 12:2 ESV

Chapter 6: Fasting Suppresses Your Flesh

1. Matthew 26:41 NKJV
2. Proverbs 1:7 NKJV
3. Ecclesiastes 7:19 NKJV
4. James 1:5-17 NKJV
5. Jeremiah 33:3 NKJV
6. Daniel 2:28 NKJV

Chapter 7: Fasting Makes You Sensitive to God

1. Romans 10:17 NKJV

Chapter 8: Fasting Strengthens Our Prayers

1. Daniel 2:22 NKJV
2. Matthew 18:20 NKJV

Chapter 9: Fasting Gets Rid of Unbelief

1. Unbelief. https://www.biblestudytools.com/dictionary/unbelief/
2. Romans 11:30, 32 NKJV
3. Hebrews 4:6,11 NKJV
4. Romans 10:17 NKJV
5. 2 Corinthians 12:10 NKJV
6. Matthew 17:17-21
7. Hebrews 11:1 NKJV

Chapter 10: Fasting Releases Supernatural Protection of God

1. Ezra 8:21-23 NKJV
2. 2 Chronicles 20:15 NKJV
3. Esther 6:6-8 NKJV
4. Ephesians 6:10 NKJV

Chapter 11: Fasting for Deliverance, Breakthrough & Destroying Strongholds

1. 2 Corinthians 10:4 NKJV
2. 2 Corinthians 10:5 NKJV
3. John 2:15-16 NKJV
4. 1 Peter 5:5-6 NKJV
5. Colossians 2:8 NIV
6. Psalm 46:10 NASB
7. John 15:4 NKJV
8. John 15:7 NKJV
9. Proverbs 16 NLT
10. Job 42:5 NLT
11. Psalm 106:13 NKJV
12. Mark 1:35 NKJV
13. John 5:19 NASB
14. Ephesians 1:3 NKJV

Chapter 12: Fasting is Spiritual Warfare

1. Ephesians 6:12 NKJV
2. Revelation 12:9 NKJV

Chapter 13: God Responds to Fasting and Prayer

1. Ezra 8:21-23 NKJV
2. John 15:7 NKJV

Chapter 14: What is Done in Private, God Will Reward Publicly

1. Matthew 6:17-18 NKJV
2. Matthew 6:1-4 NKJV

Chapter 16: Living a Fasted Life

1. Isaiah 58 NLT and NKJV
2. Luke 6:38 NKJV

Chapter 17: Fasting Will Help You Find God's Will for Your Life

1. Genesis 1:2 NKJV
2. Ephesians 5:8-11NKJV

Chapter 21: Salvation Prayer

1. John 3:3 NKJV
2. Romans 10:9-13 NKJV

Chapter 22: Personal Testimonies

1. ChristianBookProposals.Com

For more information about this book send an email to: info@advbooks.com

To purchase additional copies of this book, visit our bookstore website at www.advbookstore.com

Longwood, Florida, USA
"we bring dreams to life"™
www.advbookstore.com

www.ingramcontent.com/pod-product-compliance
Lightning Source LLC
LaVergne TN
LVHW051128080426
835510LV00018B/2299